DIGGING THE CITY

DIGGING
THE
CITY

An Urban Agriculture Manifesto

Rhona McAdam

RMB
Victoria Vancouver Calgary

Rocky Mountain Books
www.rmbooks.com

Library and Archives Canada Cataloguing in Publication

McAdam, Rhona, 1957-
    Digging the city : an urban agriculture manifesto / Rhona McAdam.

Includes bibliographical references.
Issued also in electronic formats.
ISBN 978-1-927330-22-7 (HTML).—ISBN 978-1-927330-49-4 (PDF)
ISBN 978-1-927330-21-0 (bound)

    1. Urban agriculture. I. Title.

S494.5.U72M33 2012   630.9173'2   C2012-903840-7

Printed in Canada

Rocky Mountain Books acknowledges the financial support for its publishing program from the Government of Canada through the Canada Book Fund (CBF) and the Canada Council for the Arts, and from the province of British Columbia through the British Columbia Arts Council and the Book Publishing Tax Credit.

 Canadian Heritage Patrimoine canadien   Canada Council for the Arts Conseil des Arts du Canada

 BRITISH COLUMBIA ARTS COUNCIL
Supported by the Province of British Columbia

The interior pages of this book have been produced on 100% post-consumer recycled paper, processed chlorine free and printed with vegetable-based dyes.

 FSC MIX Paper from responsible sources FSC® C016245

CONTENTS

ACKNOWLEDGEMENTS

This manifesto is less a breaking of new ground than a re-examination of the rightness of the garden. Many have led me through the jungly byways of food and agriculture, from rural to urban, field to forest, root cellar to rooftop, and everything in between.

Credit is due to all those passionate, provocative minds I have read, heard and otherwise learned from: Will Allen, Wendell Berry, Joanna Blythman, Novella Carpenter, Rachel Carson, Jonathan Safran Foer, Herbert Girardet, Ben Hewitt, Rob Hopkins, Sir Albert Howard, Sandor Ellix Katz, Tim Lang, Felicity Lawrence, Bill Mollison, Marion Nestle, Thomas F. Pawlick, Michael Pollan, Joel Salatin, Peter Singer, Tom Standage, Rudolf Steiner,

Woody Tasch, Andre Viljoen, Alice Waters, Andrew Whitley ... and so many others.

And grow, Canada! To all the local and not so local heroes who've led me down the garden path with insights and teachings of many kinds: Michael Ableman, Luanne Armstrong, Brian Brett, Sarah Elton, Bob Duncan, Corky Evans, Lee Fuge, Linda Geggie, Carolyn Herriot, Dan Jason, Mara Jernigan, Mary Alice Johnson, Lorraine Johnson, Marc Loiselle, Lorenzo Magzul, Sinclair Philip, Lana Popham, Percy Schmeiser, Jim Ternier, Sharon Rempel, Alisa Smith and J.B. MacKinnon, Wayne Roberts, Jon Steinman, Nettie Wiebe, Bob Wildfong ... and so many others.

To all the Gorge Tillicum Urban Farmers, my "neighbours growing organically"; to Elmarie Roberts and Haliburton Community Organic Farm; and to Jeanette Longfield, Kath Dalmeny, Ben Reynolds and the food warriors of Sustain, who have all proved to me the unsurpassed power in collaboration.

To the visionaries at the University of Gastronomic Sciences for diverse and incomparable opportunities to taste, question and learn. To Carlo Petrini for leading the Slow Food charge with poetry and passion. To Tom Henry for letting me explore my interests by keeping *Small Farm Canada* alive and fertile. To Canadian Organic Growers and COG-VI, LifeCycles, CR-FAIR, the Compost Education Centre, *EAT Magazine*, Transition Victoria and Glendale Gardens for generalized local enlightenment. To St. Lawrence College for letting me organize my thoughts into teachable messages for the Sustainable Local Food certificate program.

Personal thanks are due, too late, to my mother, for the suburban gardens she grew in the small towns of my youth, and for teaching me that food is worth exploring. To my good, generous and endlessly curious brothers: Steve, for his growing wisdom in the peri-urban garden; and John, for tireless assistance with whatever needs doing. To my tribe of wise women (and partners), who include Bonnie Bishop, Meli Costopoulos, Tina Couper, Leah Fritz, Ana Harland, Judy LeBlanc, Adrienne Lowden, Alice Major, Peggy Massiah, Nancy

Mattson, Mary Anne McAdam, Sue Rose, Mari-Lou Rowley and Tamar Yoseloff, for listening, planting seeds of all kinds and nourishing long friendships. To the magnificent Mary Walters I owe undying thanks for her gratifying enthusiasm and for expertly poking me with her virtual blue pencil.

This book is dedicated to all who grow, reap and nourish.

WHAT GIVES?

When I consider my Victoria backyard, wind-whipped and overshadowed by city trees, unsightly in its random pots and straggling, slug-bitten plants, I feel power. I know this garden has no hope of feeding me for a month, let alone a year, but it's partly symbolic: a piece of my ongoing protest against the forces that strangle my right to eat good food. And what also makes this feeble garden powerful is a group of neighbours who stand alongside me, sharing my fears, but also sharing their seeds and knowledge.

That sense of empowerment has been long in the making. After many years in England, I'd returned to Canada in 2002 to see my parents through their final years. By 2005 the family estate was settled; I was without a job or prospects and wondering which way to turn. Freelance writing seemed the natural course for an anchorless writer. I chose food for my subject, because I'd always liked it, and it seemed likely to hold my interest over the long term. Little did I know that, like the Chinese proverb, my chosen subject was already deep into "interesting times."

I was an innocent; a simple foodie. I liked good food; I read about it, cooked it and talked about it a lot. But when I started writing about it, I started to learn that the food system – which I, like most of us, had taken for granted – was gradually and stealthily being dismantled. I looked around in shock. I'd been in England through salmonella, BSE and foot-and-mouth scares, but always thought Canadian food was "safe."

I was startled by the extent of the food hazards listed on the Canadian Food Inspection Agency website. Food journalists were already talking about food insecurity and running the words *obesity, starvation, diabetes* and *cancer* through their headlines. The names

Monsanto and Cargill were becoming muttered profanities. Farmers were struggling to stay afloat, even with off-farm jobs to pay the bills. Genetically engineered crops, banished after ferocious public battles in Europe, appeared to have arrived in our fields and in our foods without a Canadian whisper of objection.

Just then, *The Omnivore's Dilemma* was published, and Michael Pollan laid out the problems of our age in terrifyingly simple language. The farmers were no longer feeding us: profit-driven corporations were.

At the end of 2006, I was fortunate enough to be able to drop everything and leave for a year in northern Italy, where I embarked on a master's degree in food culture and communication at the University of Gastronomic Sciences (UNISG). This was the educational arm of Slow Food, the eco-gastronomic non-profit that came into in being in Italy as a protest against fast food and has since evolved into a one-hundred-thousand-member global movement promoting food culture, tradition and biodiversity against the armies of industrial food production.

Under the tutelage of dozens of lecturers from around the world, my illusions about world food systems were smashed to bits. Lecturer after lecturer hammered home remarkably similar points from many different angles and disciplines; whether historians, geographers, anthropologists, economists, photographers, scientists, oenologists, farmers, cheese-makers, chefs or semioticians, their viewpoints were consistent. Food traditions everywhere were dying or being picked off by regulation and corporate interests, they explained. Farmland was being destroyed, contaminated, built upon; forests and family farms were being mowed under to feed livestock; oceans were being depleted, polluted and acidified. Western populations were being lulled into compliant ignorance about what their food was doing to them; and multinationals were buying up land, seeds and government interests and finding new ways to turn food into profit. Not only that: we were all living on borrowed time in a world fuelled by cheap oil and diminishing supplies of clean water and arable land.

At the end of 2007, I returned to Victoria in shock. I could not believe how ordinary and how inherently contradictory everything was. I was appalled by the food I was offered in restaurants: I simply knew too much to eat the factory-farmed beef from American feedlots, the pesticide- and antibiotic-laced prawns from Asia, the genetically modified ingredients in everything. I was stunned that people could still be driving around in SUVs, throwing the same contaminated, nutritionally bankrupt processed foods into their supermarket trolleys – while buying up supplements and pharmaceuticals to counter weight gains and food-related illnesses. They were patronizing Walmart and Costco, yet deploring the loss of their local shops and jobs. They were still spraying pesticides on their lawns and gardens, and complaining about seasonal watering restrictions designed to protect communal water supplies.

I spent the next few years trying to readjust

to a North American diet and mindset, while following up all the strands of knowledge I'd been untangling since Italy. What I learned was no more comforting than my lectures at UNISG had been. Basically, I confirmed that all those worrying niggles were building into an overwhelming body of evidence. Our food systems – our ability to grow and process foods of all kinds – were truly under attack from every direction.

The really awful fact was that there was no one enemy: the problems were systemic, interlocking and terminal. I would no sooner learn about overfishing and species extinction than changes to abattoir regulations would become a topic for study; articles on topsoil depletion fed into studies of sewage waste management; cheese-tastings descended into wrangles over government manipulation of raw milk safety issues; even a simple tour of a local family farm raised questions about pesticide residues, soil amendments, succession planning, taxation and land-use zoning. And then there were the bees.

While I was away in Italy, colony collapse disorder had started hitting the headlines in the American media. While there had been no reported cases in Canada, there were certainly massive hive losses and increases in disease. I studied beekeeping and learned about the huge impact of commercial and domestic use of pesticides on honeybees as well as other wild pollinators; I learned how climate change was affecting bees with its unpredictable cold wet spells that invited fungal infections like nosema; about the global trade in queens and the commercial use of bees in pollination, which had exacerbated the spread of varroa mites and rendered the bees too weak to fight off other infections. In short, I began to wonder how crops would be pollinated at all if we carried on destroying habitat, spraying insecticides and throwing chemical solutions at human-made problems like varroa.

I returned to Italy in 2008 to attend Terra Madre, the biennial conference of several thousand global food producers and interested parties brought together by the miracle of Slow

Food International, and there was more talk about bees. German beekeepers were buzzing. A Bavarian court order had ruled that honey made from the nectar of genetically modified crops was not only not saleable, it was not fit for human consumption and had to be destroyed. Selective breeding of honeybees was weakening their resistance to illness and contributing to the loss of bee populations that had evolved to suit their native environment. Large-scale monocrops were requiring artificial pollination – trucking honeybee hives around vast distances, or introducing bred varieties like alfalfa leafcutters – because they removed the habitat that would allow native pollinators to survive and do the pollinating work for free.

Meanwhile, in my water-rich country, issues around control of our most precious natural resource were under discussion: certain corporate interests wanted to make water a commodity rather than a human right. I started noticing how we were flushing drinking water down our toilets, and lavishing it on lawns and ornamental gardens; how water tables were falling due to poor land management and over-development; how the runoff from our roofs and driveways was eroding streambeds and washing topsoil and surface pollutants into rivers and oceans.

Confronted with water safety scares like Walkerton, questionable industrial practices leading to chemical leaks, and the excessive and polluting use of water in such activities as natural gas and potash extraction, I questioned the ethics and efficacy of regulations governing public water rights. How would we protect water for agriculture, which in large-scale irrigation is spectacularly wasteful?

But it wasn't just water: I saw waste everywhere. I saw platters of restaurant food tipped into bins destined for landfills – anaerobic dumps polluting air, soil and groundwater, where compostable waste is merged with industrial toxins and non-biodegradable materials. I saw problems in household waste disposal, where compostables and recyclables are routinely smuggled into landfills by urbanites too busy, ignorant or careless to do otherwise.

I learned about sewage waste, too: once an integral part of the cycle of food-growing, it is now contaminated by industrial chemicals and pharmaceuticals and either pumped into the ocean or handed off to farmers to spray on our produce. I saw packaging and mass consumerism crowding out common sense.

I realized that our views of time and community have become fundamentally wrong. Growing food takes time and care; so does getting to know your neighbours, with whom you share water, air and – if you're lucky – occasional meals. But, like many of the urban dwellers I'd met, I knew only a scattering of the people on my street.

It struck me that the popular wisdom of our era is that time must be saved at any cost, because corporate profit is the most important thing: more important than creating a world where all citizens can earn their daily bread. Because living wages, together with the decent working conditions past generations fought so hard to introduce, take the largest bite out of profits, as many jobs as possible – in food, agriculture and most other fields – must be mechanized out of existence, or salaries devalued to the point of penury. Wherever possible our food must be grown and produced in ways that maximize its durability, storage and profit-making potential rather than its flavour and nutrition. Feeding ourselves is no more than a necessary biological process that should ideally be executed, start to finish, in less than 30 minutes.

I was sickened to realize that we city dwellers have accepted the lie that we haven't time to feed ourselves. We've given up our right to eat good food at a pace leisurely enough to build social bonds, taste what we're eating and give ourselves time to digest it. This is one of those wrongs that Slow Food seeks to address in its mission to promote food that is good to eat, cleanly produced and fairly traded.

I was gradually connecting the dots, and realizing the vulnerability of cities like mine, teeming with citizens lulled into accepting whatever food the supermarkets chose to sell them, citizens who had turfed over their gardens or forsaken them for easy-care condominium life and who had no interest in or knowledge about growing any part of their daily diet. Who were utterly ignorant about the devastating change that looms over every aspect of our lives, with fuel and water and dwindling resources like phosphorus reaching new levels of scarcity.

And our lifestyle in Canada puts us at tremendous risk. It still shocks me to think that it's not only possible but acceptable for families to buy 100 per cent of their food from supermarkets for their entire lives. We have no control over this food: we select from what has been chosen for us, and we do so without knowing where the food comes from, how long it has travelled, who has grown and handled it on our behalf, and what risks are entailed in eating it. On Vancouver Island, where only about 5 per cent of our food is locally produced, our larger supermarkets warehouse their stock on the mainland, so we're doubly vulnerable to any disruption in our transportation systems.

But most devastatingly, the majority of us

have no idea what the ecological consequences of our food choices are, either for the people who grow the food now or for future generations who must live on the land we leave them. In buying all of our food from supermarkets, we've embraced the modern agricultural system that for 40 years has told farmers to "get big or get out."

By insisting on cheap food of questionable quality, we city-dwelling consumers have driven out of business those farmers who used to work the most productive system possible – the mixed family farm, which can potentially operate as a closed-loop, self-sufficient entity – and who carried the life-learned farming knowledge it takes to make the most of a self-contained, localized terroir. We have bought, with our cheap groceries, the expansion of family farms into mega-farms, which drive farmers to bankruptcy with their dependence on large, fossil fuel–dependent machinery; which deplete soil fertility by growing mono-crops in artificial fertilizer; which require the annual purchase of patented seeds genetically engineered to withstand larger and larger doses of purchased pesticides; and which are so large they lack habitat for pollinators and pest predators.

I wanted to get more hands-on knowledge about what all this means to my own urban food supply. So since my return from Italy I've been volunteering at Haliburton Community Organic Farm, a piece of land saved from subdivision and development by a group of concerned neighbours. Its 3.6 hectares are surrounded by houses, most of them with lawns rather than food gardens in their backyards. Not all of their occupants are in harmony with the messy business of farming; the farmers and the volunteer board that manages the farm are fully aware of the balance of interests involved in maintaining good relations. Under the watchful eyes at those windows, a group of farmers and a few volunteers grow food and teach one another what they know about ecosystems, natural pest control, organic standards, biodiversity, seed-saving, pruning, propagating and marketing fresh produce – basically, all those hard-earned moments of knowledge, care and sheer graft that add up to the not inexpensive price of well-produced food.

One thing I've learned close-up at Haliburton is that we really don't know how to acknowledge the importance of food-growing in our busy preoccupied cities. The actual cost of our food, as has been said endlessly over the past decade, is well hidden from consumers, who shop by price point, as supermarket culture has taught us to do.

And that's a powerful lesson I've learned from my own garden, too. Until you have built raised beds; installed watering systems; shredded your leaves and dug manure and nurtured your compost; scheduled and planned your plantings; obtained your seeds; started and transplanted your seedlings; erected supports for your plants; designed protection against wind and damp; gone mano-a-mano with slugs, birds, blight, drought, scale, snails, raccoons, cutworms, aphids, squirrels, hail, caterpillars, wireworms, windstorms, leaf miners and downy mildew – all for the privilege of harvesting what you've planted, fed and watered – you don't have the foggiest idea how much time and knowledge food production takes.

And you can, just possibly, be forgiven for thinking a bag of fresh lettuce really is worth only a buck or two in the middle of winter. But in our expensive lives, if food isn't cheap, then what gives? How can we – the ever-burgeoning urban masses – afford to live sustainably in Canadian cities? The answers are going to be as complex and varied as the systems that created the problems, but I believe that urban agriculture is one crucial part of the solution.

URBAN ANSWERS

In the summer of 2008, a few months after I returned from Italy, I happened upon a notice in my community association newsletter. It was addressed to anyone interested in meeting others in the area to discuss food security. I was pretty sure "food security" was what I was working toward, but – like many people I've spoken to – I had a shaky understanding of what the term meant. It sounds like food safety, but it's really about being secure in your access to an adequate food supply. In today's cities, where we rely 100 per cent on others to provide what we eat, food security is a central if largely undiscussed concern.

Since I always enjoy a new worry to chew on, I duly went along to a meeting at a neighbour's house, where I squeezed into the living room with about 15 others, and found myself in the midst of a community of food-loving folk. Some were seasoned gardeners, some complete novices and others campaigners for urban chickens or community gardens. There was a friendly mix of good nature and sound advice, and a shared passion to learn more about food production in our area. From those early meetings a movement was born.

Before too long we had a name – the Gorge Tillicum Urban Farmers, or GTUF – and have gone on to acquire a regular meeting space in our community centre, a steering committee, a small lending library and a membership that gently climbs upwards, currently numbering about 85 households. Our e-mail list lets us spread the word about anything from global food security issues to local deals on compost; from seasonal planting advice to organic pest control. Our monthly meetings are a forum for sharing food-related concerns, information about growing food in our region, and treats from our gardens. They attract upwards of 30 people from our area and beyond. Topics range from garden tools to permaculture design, and we swap seeds and seedlings that are acclimatized to our local growing conditions.

What strikes me after these meetings is that the most important crop we can harvest from urban agriculture is community, for without a sense of connection to our neighbours and the land we share, there can be no food security. We need to be able to speak to one another before we can share knowledge, skills and food. Luckily, food has always brought people together, as it has now in my neighbourhood.

Much more than the gardening club it might first appear to be, this group has shown me ways to bring food into our urban lives that reinforce the lost strands of community. Our churches may be emptying, but there are plenty of us on our knees in backyard gardens, and many of us are out there praying for just the kind of help and guidance that GTUF members can offer one another.

One thing I've discovered since joining GTUF is that we are far from alone in our quest for food security. In just about any

Canadian city you can name, you'll find practical examples: community gardens, SPIN (Small Plot Intensive) Farming (a.k.a. lawn or backyard farming), Community-supported Agriculture (CSA) schemes, farmers' markets, school gardens and community education in planting, growing and preserving your own foods. Transition Towns, the seedlings of a movement started in England, are blossoming across Canada. Intended to build communities that can survive the end of cheap oil without waiting for governments to grind into gear, Transition Initiatives always include food security efforts.

Though government policies always lag behind immediate needs, municipalities are more nimble than provincial or federal agencies. They're "on the ground" with the practicalities of running cities, and ensuring they can feed their populations is something they're starting to take very seriously. Food security is starting to work its way through the political levels in the form of urban food policies – Toronto and Vancouver each have one; other municipalities are working on them as I write. These policies address the urgent needs of hungry citizens, the many food-related aspects of public health, and community-building projects like community gardens, community kitchens and local markets. They also include bylaws that regulate the production and distribution of local food. Whether you believe we need legislative frameworks or grassroots action or both, urban agriculture is finding its place in the collective consciousness as a means of making our cities more food secure.

It's natural to look for models, and anything that works in urban centres in developing countries – where much of the groundwork has been done – will have some application in Canada. We can also look back, particularly to the success of Victory Gardens, which encouraged home owners to plant food gardens to help to feed our country during the First and Second World Wars. So seriously were we committed back then that in 1918 Victoria passed municipal legislation allowing the seizure of urban land for purposes of food production.

But we were still relatively close to the land at that time and had a crisis to spur such decisive action.

Nowadays, there is one particular model to which all discussions of urban agriculture eventually point, and that's Cuba. Havana's *organopónicos*, or organic urban gardens, are amazing achievements and shining examples of adaptability, but as models they come with cautions. They were established after the Soviet Union's 1990 collapse abruptly ended Cuban oil imports. This in turn collapsed Cuba's agricultural industry, which like ours today was totally dependent on oil-fuelled machinery and artificial (oil-based) fertilizers and pesticides. Food shortages swiftly brought the country's population literally to the point of starvation.

In order to feed its population, Cuba turned to small-scale organic methods of growing, using every available scrap of land within and outside cities. The country's state farms were broken up into co-operatives. By 2003 farmers had converted over three hundred thousand backyard patios to gardens, setting up compost-enriched container gardens on paved or infertile areas. There were economic benefits to abandoning industrial farming, too: the production of bio-pesticides has saved the Cuban economy $15 million annually. It's an inspiring example, but not a complete solution in a country that still imports 70 per cent of its food supply.

The return to natural farming methods in Cuba was only made possible by tapping the knowledge of the dwindling population of a traditional farming generation. Invaluable as that knowledge was, it isn't guaranteed to filter reliably onward through the generations: currently much of the urban farming in Havana is done by older/retired people; as in most Westernized economies, younger people work in office jobs to bring home needed cash. Even in this model of agricultural revival, it seems that farming isn't viewed as a lucrative or attractive livelihood by the younger generation.

Cuba did manage to restructure its food supply to meet its immediate needs, but it is hard to say how applicable this approach would be here in Canada. We differ from Cuba in our capitalistic views of employment, our multi-national-owned food and seed supply, and our policy of private land ownership. And – so far, at least – we lack the urgency of a fuel crisis to propel citizens to action.

In a sense, this is liberating: we can learn from and adapt what's been done in the wider world, but we must create our own models, which meet our own unarticulated crises.

In order to teach a community to feed itself, you must first have a community. But if there's anything that Canadian cities have in common, it's the lack of cohesive community in their neighbourhoods. Within a few decades of urbanization and the migratory patterns of boom and bust economies, it's become per-fectly acceptable to live surrounded by people whose names you don't know.

One of the great things a community group like the Gorge Tillicum Urban Farmers does is give its members a reason and vehicle to meet their neighbours. GTUF meetings are neutral territory: we're brought together by a common interest in a subject that touches every living creature on the planet. I don't pretend that all 85 households in GTUF are now firm friends; indeed there are many members I've never met. But it's a precious connection that gives us common ground when we're ready to reach out.

Food-safe Cities

Food security may be misread as food safety, but it's not an unconnected term, as you cannot be food-secure until your food is safe. A trawl through the Canadian Food Inspection Agency's alerts, regularly published on its website, yields a hair-raising smorgasbord of undeclared milk and nuts, suspected salmonella in chili powder and peppermint tea, E. coli in luncheon meats and dog food, and listeria in processed cheese slices. The overwhelming majority of these contaminations are the result of our large, centralized, food systems. When foods are produced in large quantities, it becomes easier for one small mistake to become a calamity because contamination can spread into large numbers of products. And when they're produced in a centralized factory and shipped around a large country, it can be very hard to contain the problem.

So I'd argue that cities should not rely exclusively on foods imported from large centralized processors but should instead develop more local sources of food. This means attending to the sources of agricultural products, spending time, money and political will to protect agricultural land around our cities – as British Columbia does with variable success through its Agricultural Land Reserve, and Ontario struggles to do with the greenbelts around Ottawa and Toronto. Cities must fight tooth and nail for these regional and provincial land policies. Municipalities have a vested interest in promoting locally produced foods in order to create viable local food economies, improve local food safety and work toward an abundant food future.

It's important, too, to turn our thoughts to producing and processing more of our food within the city limits, where so much private land could be turned to agricultural use. Small-scale food producers are already serving many of us well, their wares appearing at farmers' markets and filling the shelves of "buy local" specialty shops. One of the Gorge Tillicum Urban Farmers has even managed to scale the bylaw hurdles and sell produce and preserves from a farm stand outside her home.

Culture and Food

Many lost food preparation skills could restore to home kitchens the craft of transforming and preserving the harvest. The popularity of classes in topics like bread-making, cheese-making, fermented foods and home canning suggests that many urbanites are willing to resume control and are hungry for the know-how. Community kitchens exist in most cities, but most urbanites are unaware of them, or of the benefits of communal cooking as a way to share skills and ingredients.

Canadian urbanites are from many different cultural backgrounds, and so are their eating habits. Our famously multicultural nation, in principle at least, embraces many food traditions, for food is one of the central aspects of cultural identification. At the same time, we've become a well-travelled nation, and we've brought home our love of tropical and exotic foods: mangoes, papayas and lemongrass were once unknowns that now find a place on most urban grocery shelves.

However, if we insist on enjoying the varied diet that we've come to take for granted, and if we would like every immigrant group in Canada to have access to its traditional foods, we commit ourselves to an unsustainable global food system.

Many foods to which different cultures are attached simply cannot be grown or produced in Canada. Most of us could, if forced, live without mangoes and coconuts and almonds. But diets built around plantain or cassava or lotus root – or even rice – perpetuate a demand for imports and a dependence on fossil-fuel-powered transport.

Moreover, we pay little heed to the social and economic conditions under which exotic fruits and vegetables are produced for our consumption – very few Canadians buy fairly traded products of any kind. Where these crops are grown for export markets, it may well be at the cost of a local economy's ability to feed its own people. I think that we, as global citizens, need to question whether we really have the right to purchase whatever we want just because we are in the privileged position of being able to pay for it.

At the very least we should be able to offer a culturally diverse population the choice not to eat foods that are proscribed by cultural, religious or dietary restrictions. Pork – or even meat in general – is a good starting point, but even that may be hidden in some foods. The lard concealed in pastry might not be recognized or declared as a pork product; neither might Phospholipase A2, an enzyme developed for use in commercial bread as a crumb softener, whose source is a pig's pancreas.

People who do not wish to consume or cannot digest milk products might be surprised to find them turning up in everything from granola bars to vinegar to luncheon meats and sausages. Consumers have no way of knowing what animal or plant is the source of the DNA inserted into genetically modified foods, nor, unless they are food chemists, of understanding the source of many of the chemical preservatives, colourants and flavourings listed on our food labels.

You might argue that some of these are niggling examples, at least to those who have no cultural restrictions around food. But they will offend, and in some cases harm, the unsuspecting consumer who adheres to a restrictive diet. The only way to be sure you are eating what you think you are eating, after all, is to take your own food preparation entirely in hand, starting with growing the raw ingredients. This is a challenge when we've mostly given up home cooking in favour of what we can pick up readymade from supermarkets and takeouts – the foods that make up the notorious Western diet.

We can't say that the Western diet – processed foods high in saturated fats, simple carbohydrates, sugars and salts, and lacking fibre and nutrients – actually serves any culture well, since it harms everyone who eats it, and "Western diet" is really a misnomer. It would be more accurately known as the Convenience Food Diet. It is real city food, designed to relieve urbanites of the onerous task of fuelling a human body.

First Nations communities, like the rest of us, have found that the Western diet, combined with a sedentary lifestyle, creates disastrously high levels of food-related health conditions. Type 2 diabetes, heart disease and obesity, as well as diseases of the gallbladder and certain cancers, have all been linked to this toxic combination.

On Vancouver Island, projects such as the Feasting for Change program – which brings First Nations Elders together with young people to teach traditional food skills – adopt elements of traditional diets and teaching skills to cultivate, harvest and prepare traditional indigenous foods. These are proving helpful not just in improving community health, but in restoring the cultural ties that come from sharing food and its traditions.

After all, from the fundamental animal need to eat came the refinements of culture: manners, customs, rituals around eating. It's no coincidence that grassroots action so often takes place around the potluck supper meeting. Sharing food – no matter what your food culture – brings us back to that nurturing of community. What we've lost in the way of food preparation skills can in fact be restored by communal cooking and eating: community kitchens, grassroots cooking classes and even potluck dinners can help.

Nutrients, Nutrition and Nutritionism

People who live alone – over a quarter of Canada's population, according to the 2006 census – are very likely not spending their evenings cooking nutritionally sound, well-balanced meals for one. Nor do seniors on tight budgets have the reason or resources to cook healthy meals; they risk ending up in care when their nutritionally starved brains and bodies finally stop working. Children raised on foods that fail to nurture brain and body will face diminishing health and intelligence throughout their lifetimes. The answer to these deficiencies is more likely to be found in community-based cooking and food-growing programs than by turning to science for answers to problems that science helped create.

Clearly the convenience foods – carefully and scientifically labelled with nutritional content and polysyllabic ingredients – that make up the Western diet are not nourishing. Meeting a recommended daily calorie intake is not the same as taking in the nutrients needed for good health. Take a spin round any "food court" in any shopping mall in Canada; you are usually forced to make choices between what Anthony Bourdain calls the King, the Clown and the Colonel: degrees of fast food that are soaked in oil and laced with sugar and salt. Whole grains have been stripped of their nutrients and returned to the table as pale additive-rich carbs, ready for the deep fryer or paired with factory-farmed meats. Salads are accompanied by dressings that are astronomically high in fat, sugar and salt, while fresh fruits and vegetables were likely grown in exhausted soils, picked too early, shipped too far and stored too long to be nutritionally valuable.

We need alternatives to these foods. Locally grown foods are fresher and therefore taste and keep better than well-travelled supermarket produce. Armed with fresh delicious ingredients, we can create a population with a taste for real food, that knows and cares how it's grown or prepared and will refuse to accept a "nutrient delivery system" in its place. This is where school gardens can kick in, to instil a new food ethic in the kids who plant, grow, harvest and prepare their own foods as part of their school curriculum.

Food learning starts in childhood. Foods we have grown up with might seem safe and healthy, because we've always eaten them. But in fact those foods aren't necessarily the same as they were even a quarter-century ago. Nutritional values in commercial crops have been declining for years; sugar content in fruits has been bred upwards.

Our recipes tell another dangerous tale: no general-audience cookbook published in the last 50 or 60 years includes meatless main courses, aside from maybe macaroni and cheese: that job was left to vegetarians and religious or ethnic cuisines. Canadian meat consumption has now reached record levels, and so have our food-related health problems. As a culture we have abandoned the cycling of feast and fast that governed intake of meat products in a more functional religious age.

We need to check out the new religions that vegans, raw foodists and the Meatless Monday campaigns offer as healthful alternatives and positive action against the myriad issues surrounding commercial meat production: greenhouse-gas emissions, pollution of air and water, meat adulteration, animal cruelty and the harmful effects on health of consuming too much animal protein. Alternative protein sources and small-scale meat production are possibilities that urban agriculture can bring home to Canadians.

A Question of Scale – and Distance

It must be obvious to the idlest bystander that today's corporate-led food production machine is unsustainable. For growing, watering, processing and transporting food, producing one calorie of food costs us anywhere from a 7:1 to a 10:1 ratio in energy consumed. And where the calories burned to produce our food come from finite and increasingly costly energy sources, we are doing more than running an energy deficit: we are heading full-tilt toward disaster.

But we can turn that buggy around. We can take charge of our own food supply and choose to understand how our food is produced, where it comes from, and how to make best use of it.

Small-scale organic agriculture can help feed our bulging urban populations. It can be done within cities themselves. It's much cheaper to set up than large-scale agriculture, and it's many times more energy-efficient and productive. We can develop food systems that are not totally dependent on fossil fuels to produce and power farming equipment and distribution vehicles, and provide and process the raw materials for fertilization, pesticides, packaging and equipment.

The environmental payoff is there, as well: small-scale organic agriculture is not so vulnerable to large-scale monocrop failures through extremes of weather or single-minded pests; topsoil loss and erosion of lands ploughed for large-scale production; stress on the water table caused by large-scale irrigation; eutrophication of rivers and oceans from fertilizer runoff; loss of habitat for native pollinators and their integrated ecosystems; interference with drainage and wetlands affecting soil fertility and carbon capture; increased use of chemical pesticides in "conservation" (no-till) farming; accidental contamination of conventional and organic crops like canola and soybeans by genetically modified ones.

Small-scale food processing is desirable not just because of food safety. The size of the industrial-scale facilities required for mass production of cheap food makes them costly to heat, cool and clean; these three activities require prolific quantities of fuel and water. Fuel and water are increasingly precious and can be better controlled in smaller operations. Small-scale production means smaller-scale waste and refuse.

Producing the food nearer its market creates efficiencies of transport that are not possible for a global marketing system with its complex logistics and elaborately calculated formulae. We can avoid the need for special packaging and chemical (gas) treatment and/or chilling; we can reduce our reliance on long-haul transport methods that even at their most efficient consume breathtaking quantities of fuel and are responsible for 20 per cent of Canada's CO_2 emissions. In my neighbourhood, Deb, a SPIN farmer, picks produce from the backyard and carries it out to a table in front of her house; people can walk to Deb's farm stand, put a couple of kilos of food in their bag and walk home with it.

One thing we can work on with local and small-scale production is improving the way food is distributed around our cities. Most of us have heard the term "food deserts" by now: those areas of an urban centre where access to food is restricted to convenience foods, non-perishables and fast-food outlets, rather than nutritious foods including fresh fruit and vegetables. But upscale neighbourhoods, too, are often designed without food services. In these neighbourhoods it doesn't much matter whether food is within walking distance (it seldom is) or within reach of public transportation (low-density, upper-echelon housing developments don't have the population to support it) because residents are assumed to have private vehicles to drive to malls and markets. But with a diminishing supply of increasingly costly fuel, here as in so many areas, we need to plan for food distribution that is not reliant on cheap fossil fuel.

Most of Canada's residential neighbourhoods – and our city streets and parks – are typically landscaped with lawns and inedible ornamentals. How little it would take to replace cedar hedges, plane trees, horse chestnuts and elms with berry bushes and fruit or edible-nut trees whose bounty could be harvested by or for the needy, keeping food firmly in the public eye. In cities like Victoria, Vancouver, Edmonton and Toronto, fruit-picking projects encourage homeowners to bring in non-profit societies to pick and distribute unwanted fruit to food security projects within the community.

Year-Round Cheap Food Is Expensive

The most serious problem in achieving food security, worldwide but also within cities, is how we equalize the cost and availability of good food. In order to bring more fresh fruit and vegetables into food banks and other food distribution projects, "grow a row" programs are springing up to encourage home gardeners to plan for the needs of their community when they sow their gardens. The Gorge Tillicum Urban Farmers distribute their surplus via a couple of community kitchens. Good Food Box programs that offer fresh produce for affordable prices have grown up in urban centres large and small across the country, bringing high-quality food within the economic reach of lower-income consumers. It's going to take some serious lateral thinking to swing the balance around and make good food more widely accessible.

But we also need to integrate a national food trade to assure a year-round supply of good fresh food. We live in a very large, climatically challenging country that is simply not suited to growing all food types in all regions through all seasons. It follows that if we want to continue eating wheat and cooking in canola oil, we must depend on the prairies, whose growing climate is suited to production of these grains. If we want seafood, we must depend on our coastal waters to go on producing. If we want fruit, we must support local growers in our fruit belts and help them to preserve the orchards that are being torn up to make way for more lucrative enterprises like vineyards and real estate development. If we want our northern communities to eat balanced diets, we must continue shipping food from the southern farmlands to supply their needs.

And if we must have mangoes, avocados, pineapples and bananas, or any other fresh fruits in the winter, all of which our supermarkets are happy to provide, we go on supporting global trade, with all its associated inequities and environmental costs.

Supermarkets – growing up as they did with the motorized lifestyle, thanks to cheap oil, of course – have contributed to the destruction of our small shops, our family businesses and our downtown cores. Knowing the public would come to them, developers have set up massive retail complexes only accessible by car, where items are bought in such volume that you need a car to take them home. Canadians' addiction to Walmarts and Costcos and big-box stores of all kinds has wooed them away from the retailers next door, and taught them to buy everything – most damagingly food – on the basis of price alone.

Few of us realize how little it takes to kill off a local business – and the livelihood of the families who work there. According to the New Economics Foundation, which studied the matter in Britain, it only takes half the residents doing a third of their shopping at the new box store to kill off local shops. But we can turn this around if we relearn how to support our local businesses. We have been brainwashed into forgetting how much power our consumer dollar holds, and we need to start putting our money where our mouths are when it comes to buying good quality food.

WHERE THE
SEED FALLS

Well. There's no doubt the food security problems we're facing, whether in cities or not, are
monumental: a tsunami of engineered unsus-
tainability. But there are many hopeful food
solutions cresting in our cities, and I think it's
possible to turn the food security tide within
our lifetime.

Urban agriculture discussions tend to
divide between urban farming – growing food
in cities for profit – and backyard growing,
where homeowners aim to produce food for
themselves or for charity. But there are many
shared concerns, areas of overlap and common
approaches when facing the challenges of
growing food in cities.

School Gardens

A lot of the best ideas start with children. It might be too late to change the minds and habits of some adults, but kids can learn new ways to create community that will see them into adulthood, and – who knows? – maybe save the planet at the same time.

Educational institutions of all kinds – kindergartens, schools, colleges and universities – are ideal platforms for food-production projects. Whether they're growing food for snacks, or a cooking class, or to supply the cafeteria or a chef training program, school gardens can teach students how to plan, tend and harvest. They can teach valuable lessons about container gardens, soil and water stewardship, local growing conditions and composting methods.

There was a lot of interest in this through the noughties; whether it will continue is anyone's guess. One of the fundamental problems with school growing programs is that they have to run over the academic year, which, as far as the plants are concerned, starts at harvest and ends at planting times. Someone needs to keep the worm bins alive and the plants watered and weeded over the summer if the lessons are to continue in the fall. Moreover, curriculum planning is subject to the whims of political change and the contingencies of funding, both of which can change overnight.

Perhaps adding a commercial dimension is the key to keeping older students interested, as in the example set by Toronto high school Bendale Business and Technical Institute with its garden market. It met the challenge of scarce student labour during the summer by tapping grant money to pay students to tend the garden over the summer and sell the produce at an on-site farmers' market.

Altruistic goals can also work, as with programs in which students raise food for food banks, soup kitchens or disadvantaged groups. But I think the best approach integrates the garden with the rest of the curriculum: using food-growing to demonstrate principles of mathematics, chemistry, biology – and all subjects, really, for there is nothing in human life and culture that is not touched in some way by food. Combining school gardens with community initiatives would be even better; perhaps there is a way to link them with community gardens and gardeners.

Community Gardens

"Community garden" is a dual-purpose term. It can mean a garden that is jointly cared for by a group or committee in a community; or it might be used to describe allotment gardens that are run by public or community organizations.

Community gardens – in the first sense of the term – are excellent ways to use gardening to build community, by educating and inspiring. A garden can bring members of its community together to work on growing projects or maintain a collective source of food in an urban neighbourhood. The purpose may be to raise food for the community, or to bring a community together to raise food for donation. But unless there is a formal structure in place – which can be off-putting to the livelier participants – it may be hard to keep the momentum going and the garden tended.

Such a place is often the brainchild of a single person, and as members cycle in and out of neighbourhoods, so the energy flows in and out of community projects. Gardens are no different from any other community project or land tenancy in this way. They can be scuppered by a change of neighbours or a change in land use or other regulations. Some gardens thrive on borrowed ground – vacant lots are often freed up for community purposes – but in times of economic boom, the landowners are likely to choose profit or politics over potatoes, and many gardens have been lost to development.

Allotment gardens are well-established in Europe, particularly in England, where they have existed for centuries, and where since 1887 municipal governments have been obliged by law to provide them to their citizens. Even so, British allotment gardens have been on the wane – in both size and numbers – since the end of the Second World War, when population gains put housing and other construction at a higher priority for land use. With the revived interest in food security, however, waiting lists for allotments have been surging, and it's not uncommon for gardeners to have to wait several years to get their hands into English soil.

Here in Canada, we may struggle to find room in our newfangled urban lives for an old-world concept like this – particularly one that requires constant care and attention in a lifestyle that is riddled with distractions and competing interests. In our private-backyard world we haven't the allotment culture that shows us what to do or how to behave in a shared space; we haven't the older generation of allotment gardeners handing on the knowledge and interest. But interest is growing nonetheless, and so are the waiting lists for Canadian plots.

Urban allotment gardens can be training grounds where knowledge and techniques are passed down from more experienced allotment-holders. They offer a rare opportunity to make community connections and learn to share a communal growing space with others.

These gardens require careful planning around issues like whether to allow chemical pesticides and fertilizers, which may affect neighbouring plots; or how to manage the water supply; or whether to include features like public toilets and security lights. In our urban gardens, it's a sad reality that there will be vandalism and theft; many community gardeners know and try to plan for this, by leaving sacrificial crops near the boundaries, or by growing unusual crops unlikely to be lifted.

We are not yet at the point of desperation at which community food production takes top priority in our busy, demanding, city lives. Many allotment plots are abandoned when life overtakes ambition. Every allotment garden project plans for this falling-off. But with it falls the power and momentum of community food production. Gardens cannot simply be picked up midway through the season as they become available, particularly in Canadian cities, where the climate forces a short growing season and soils take time to build up – as do gardening skills.

At present, allotment gardening in Canada is too often a luxury, practiced by those who know how to lobby for change, who can afford to rent a space and buy the tools and trappings, and, most important, who can already afford to eat.

There are exceptions, of course: community groups in lower-income neighbourhoods can give disenfranchised growers a head start. But it usually takes money – typically grant money, which means grant-writers, as well – to secure the land, to test and rebuild the soil, to put in fencing, planters and irrigation, and to buy tools. Or it takes hugely committed volunteers who can cultivate enough community good-will to do all these things at no financial cost. Gardens set up by community groups to teach growing skills can also teach the skills needed to find, secure and maintain allotment plots in other areas.

But the future of community and allotment gardens is only as secure as the winds of public opinion. Sustainability and its associated concepts – like food security – are already starting to feel a bit worn and overexposed in the media, regardless of their actual urgency. For those who have the means and desire to go on living the comfortable life they're used to, and have no interest in making optional lifestyle changes, the uprooting of perfectly good parking lots and neighbourhood parks is objectionable.

A couple of recent proposals for community gardens in Vancouver were stalled by neighbours wanting to have green space left as park land. The answer of the garden advocates was to hold more community meetings, since the objections must have come from people who didn't understand the principles well enough.

I wonder if that is so. What if these people understand the principles perfectly and just don't see the point, since they do not plan to make use of the growing spaces? Or if they see the gardens as the playgrounds of the green elite? For all the talk out there about the growing threat to food security for all of us, a powerfully large number of shoppers are shopping just as they have for a decade or more, and show not the slightest interest in growing any of their own food.

Life is complicated in our cities. It's busy. We could be occupied full time just handling our e-mail, texts, blogs, tweets and apps, going to work, watching TV and having some down time. Realistically, few adults of working age will be willing to shoehorn unpaid food-growing time into their agendas, certainly not while our governments are failing to put food security on the public agendas.

But the effects of climate change on food production are already reflected in food prices. Climate-created shortages, coupled with escalating populations, mean that food will become less available, even to the well off. We would all be wise to learn some food-growing skills to pad our menus. Community and allotment gardens are among the best ways to acquire those skills.

Front-yard gardens

"Urban agriculture" brings to mind neat squares of green vegetables growing in every backyard. In fact, the best urban agriculture opportunities integrate a number of growing methods and food sources, and are public enough to inspire others. The front yard – for too long the domain of water-hungry imported turf grass, larded with artificial fertilizers and herbicides – is a great place to plant your edible badge of honour.

But we have lawns for a reason: they're really easy to take care of, and they survive a fair amount of neglect. Moreover, we're living in a time when a neat front yard is one of the things you need in order to be considered a good neighbour. Violating that norm is to break new ground, literally and figuratively. The neighbourhood values and municipal regulations may take time to catch up with the sometimes slovenly appearance of food security made real.

Still, whether you're tearing up your front lawn or covering it with containers, you can make a good example of yourself, meet your neighbours and share your bounty by making food visible and accessible. You can be subtle, too: edible landscaping is, I think, the niche market of choice for today's gardeners. Food plants can be as beautiful as the imported ornamentals that make up 90 per cent of urban gardens, and kitchen garden designs can rival their inedible counterparts for lush artistry.

Native plant gardens can easily accommodate edible plant species suitable for your climate, easy on water and impervious to the pests and diseases that plague imported varieties. Better yet, in these bee-challenged times, native plants are timed to feed pollinators a well-orchestrated diet throughout the growing season. Learning about traditional plant uses in your region can open up a whole new world of knowledge: suddenly your garden can become a source of food, medicine, teas and condiments, as well as pride and beauty.

Backyard gardens

If your best food-growing space is in your backyard, you might still rile some of your unenlightened neighbours. Any population includes a wide range of food-growing abilities and interests; tolerance and understanding are necessary if urban agriculture is to flourish.

Lantzville, BC, couple Dirk and Nicole Becker made national headlines in 2010, when their urban farm business was threatened with closure after the neighbours complained. The Beckers are a lesson to us all. Their two-and-a-half-acre property is hardly what most city-dwellers would call urban, but regulations follow boundary creep and reflect the changing values of an urbanizing population. We need to nourish tolerance and enlightenment in our municipal governments, as well as a commitment to encouraging urban agriculture projects both public and private.

Up on the Roof

Green roofs or rooftop gardens are often mooted as ways to improve air quality and building insulation, and offer a useful option for food production in cities. Most Canadian cities are moving to include green-roof policies in their city planning: Toronto's green-roof regulations for new buildings came into force in 2009.

For several reasons, few green-roof projects

actually include food production. Raising food gardens above ground level introduces technical problems – start talking soil-based growing on roofs and you enter a nether world of building permits, structural loads, weight distribution, building height and wind load increases. At a minimum, you'll have to reinforce an existing roof to bear the weight of soil, and then consider what effect foot traffic and equipment like wheelbarrows and tools will have on the roofing cover; figure out how you'll get materials, supplies and workers up to the roof, and the harvest back down; and also come up with a plan for power and water supply as well as drainage and disposal of garden waste. And deal with rats, who are great climbers; and crows and gulls, who are great foragers.

This is not to say that rooftop growing is impossible. Container gardens are probably the most practical method, as Montreal's Rooftop Garden Project has demonstrated in its dozen or so productive food gardens around the city, covering rooftops and balconies in self-watering containers.

Down on the Ground

Canadian cities have not been designed with a lot of green space, and what is there tends to be covered in lawns, flower gardens and ornamental shrubs and trees that are easy to maintain. The growing demand in cities for edible ornamentals in public spaces is meeting some resistance from city officials, who cite liabilities (people slipping on dropped fruit, for example) and pest issues.

The fruit and nuts that are grown don't have to be wasted through ignorance: urbanites can learn to distinguish edible from non-edible chestnuts, or discover that such varieties as monkey-puzzle trees produce edible nuts. Guerrilla gardeners are arming themselves with knowledge about fruit propagation, and threatening to graft fruit-bearing branches onto ornamental trees, which is a happy thought.

Meanwhile, lawns everywhere are being put to better use. SPIN Farming is one of the commercial ways to produce food in cities, using a number of backyards or other spaces.

SPIN farmers enter into contracts with homeowners to grow cash crops in underused spaces, and may agree to pay for the tenancy in cash, farming tax relief and/or produce. A business model and growing philosophy that started in Saskatoon, it's proving a popular way for urban farmers in the US, Canada, Australia, the UK, Ireland, the Netherlands and South Africa to get the land they need to start farming businesses. Backyard-sharing databases across the country help to match farmers with homeowners, and time and experience are making the process of leasing those lawns more orderly.

It's a practice that does have pitfalls, of course. When a farmer strikes an agreement with one homeowner, there may come a time when the property is sold to someone who wants a lawn or multi-family dwelling rather than a row of greens. Land tenure, that agricultural bugbear, strikes in city and country alike.

Like any tenant farmer, a SPIN farmer will adjust the crops to the security of the tenure.

You will not find perennials – raspberries, blueberries, tree fruits – in a SPIN farmer's repertoire unless they exist already in the homeowner's garden.

In Water or Under Glass

Greenhouses are one way of extending growing seasons and can be used in spaces that are covered with concrete or contaminated soil. They are a growing agricultural concern in a country that wants fresh tomatoes, peppers and cucumbers year-round. Between 2002 and 2006, commercial operations increased 39 per cent to cover 1092 hectares of Canadian land in greenhouses (that's equivalent to about 1,750 Canadian football fields).

Growing from soil (geoponics) rather than in one of the soilless alternatives is thought to provide the best nutritional payback. This can involve planting in the soil floor of the greenhouse – a popular method for greenhouses that are moved periodically for crop rotation purposes – or in bags of peat or soil-based growing media.

Hydroponics – the most popular commercial application, and one that enables rooftop greenhouse growing – relies upon a water-based medium to supply nutrients, but it doesn't always mean the roots of the plants are suspended in a liquid medium: they can be supported by inert materials that are in many cases anything but natural. These might include perlite or vermiculite (volcanic rock or minerals, superheated to form pebbles), mineral wool or rockwool (heated, spun volcanic rock, limestone and coke), gravel or clay pebbles dipped in nutrient solution (aggregate substrate). These inert materials are typically discarded and replaced after two or three years. Though not considered toxic materials, many of them require considerable energy in production and are problematic to dispose of in any quantity.

A third method, aeroponics, involves misting or spraying plant roots with a nutrient solution. An offshoot of this method is called fogponics. Like hydroponics, these methods require a great commitment to plastic for irrigation and planters, plus power, artificial light and heat, and more inert materials to support the plants.

In the case of hydroponics or aeroponics, growers need to buy plant nutrients, which means breaking the cycle of self-sufficient growing. Moreover, unless the nutrients are recycled or reprocessed in some way, such greenhouse operations risk contaminating groundwater and other water sources when they are disposed of. If the hydroponic greenhouse is using one of the inert materials as a growing medium, a disposal problem arises.

The bumblebees that are bought in to pollinate commercial greenhouses have carried diseases to the wild population, bringing two species to the brink of extinction in recent years; the Asian lady beetles (also called Japanese ladybugs or Harlequin lady beetles) brought in to deal with aphids are now outcompeting native lady beetle species.

Greenhouses are artificial means of growing, and it takes energy to build and heat them. Greenhouses covered in plastic sheeting, which are also known as "hoop-houses," can be made for three to five hundred dollars from polyfilm and plastic or metal tubing. But plastic sheeting is, of course, energy-intensive to produce and does not biodegrade (if it did, it would not be much use, of course!). It must be replaced – depending on its weight and the growing conditions – every couple of years or so.

Finding somewhere to recycle the degraded plastic sheeting is tricky, not least because it is used in such large quantities. A study of agricultural plastics in Saskatchewan found that the province used some 239,967 square metres of greenhouse plastic, enough to cover nearly 30 Canadian football fields; if the plastic is replaced every three years, that amounts to 11.33 tonnes of recyclable polyethylene, and that's before domestic, industrial and other agricultural plastics – twine, plastic mulches and the like – are factored in. And that's just one province. That's a lot of recycling, and a lot of landfill.

Glass greenhouses are at least made of materials that can be recycled, and are more durable, but they are very costly to manufacture, buy and repair, and they are not as portable as their plastic counterparts. Home gardeners can recycle old windows and glass doors to build them. This kind of low-tech construction may be one of the great untapped small businesses of the future.

Heated greenhouses, used to grow vegetables through cold winters, are highly energy intensive. Unheated greenhouse growing, using methods popularized by Maine farmer Eliot Coleman, typically require use of row covers or some other method of keeping the plants above freezing; some use Christmas lights, which of course need a source of electricity.

A greenhouse is an impermeable surface, like a road or rooftop, and if it covers green space, that compounds the existing problem we have with drainage, water tables and compacted earth. One commercial hydroponics company in Delta, BC, boasts a 24.3-hectare operation. That's a lot of ground cover.

Container gardening is an adaptable and even mobile method of growing. Everything from old buckets to wading pools can be filled with dirt and placed anywhere there's enough light and water. Brooklyn's whimsical Truck Farm project shows that you can even drive around with plants growing in the back of your pickup – and run a profitable CSA (vegetable box program), as well.

Bags, Buckets and Great Big Pots

You may not have a backyard, a front yard or room for a greenhouse on your property. You may not have property at all. But the smallest of homes has at least a window, and often more – perhaps a balcony or roof terrace. And if you have one of those, you can grow something in a pot. Container gardening is one of those expanding terms that embraces just about any shape or size of planter you can imagine.

There are planters designed for apartment-dwellers that stack rows of pots along windows, so you can grow your herbs and salad and frame your view of the city at the same time. Other entrepreneurs have developed mini-greenhouses that look more like mini-bars, perfect for your micro-greens. Going even smaller, you can always make your own sprouts with no more technology than a mason jar and some cheesecloth fastened with a rubber band.

Heading in the other direction, anything that holds its shape can be used for a planter. Air bricks (breeze blocks), milk jugs, garbage cans, dinghies, buckets, burlap sacks, bathtubs, broken freezers, teapots ... and yes, even purpose-built pots and planters are well suited for growing some kind of food.

My own limited light and growing space has made me a great believer in containers. On my front steps I have two large pots that hold carrots, leeks, sorrel, radishes, arugula, nasturtiums, and, as I write, I'm about to put my winter greens – hardy lettuce and some kale and cabbage – into them. Out back, my collection includes Jerusalem artichokes looming out of recycling bins, and two children's wading pools, one planted with oca – a delicious Andean root vegetable with abundant foliage – and the other with winter radish, carrots and celeriac.

So, there are many places to grow food. Chances are that many of us can produce more than we can use ourselves, so we need to think as well about distribution.

HOW TO DELIVER IT

Alisa Smith and J.B. MacKinnon's *The 100-mile Diet* drew an arbitrary line around their Vancouver home; they vowed to eat only foods produced within that radius. Their experiment, and their book, whose title became a movement, proved wildly influential in Canada, coming at a time when people were starting to wake up to food insecurity and question the provenance of their meals. The couple lived by concepts that readers had not begun to consider: Where does my flour come from? What is it like to live without vegetable oil for a year? How would I find local eggs if I lived downtown? Does wheat grow in my area?

The project alerted us to broken strands in the local supply chain. It helped to regenerate interest in producing local food, but what it did not do was provide us with a single neat solution to cover all the complexities of building urban food systems. These are being encountered and addressed piecemeal by those involved in urban growing.

Markets, Farm Stands and Other Retail Outlets

Once urban food has been grown, there's the question of what to do with it. Today's consumers expect, in any exchange of money for goods – including food – a reliable supply of a standard quality. Urban food grown by non-standard urban farmers might be tasty, nutritious and responsibly produced, but it isn't likely to be the pretty, uniformly sized and unblemished stuff our culture expects. This trade-off – perfect appearance on the one hand and good flavour, absolute freshness and top nutritional content on the other – is something we'll need to teach ourselves to appreciate and pay for.

Many aspiring urban farmers have run smack into bylaws at this late stage. Things that aren't an issue when planting or growing suddenly become so when harvest time comes and hungry neighbours start asking if they can buy produce. The problems arise from the rules of the market economy, the ways that consumers have been trained to shop, and the efforts by governments to enforce various regulations and keep our food supply safe and reliable.

One area where cities often have trouble catching up with local trends is policies around who can sell food. Our food supply is barricaded behind food safety policies designed to protect us from unscrupulous commerce and the health perils of large-scale agri-food enterprises.

There are, however, often small holes through which backyard growers can fit, as long as they don't bandy certifiable terms like "organic" or "fair trade" around, and as long as they don't try to involve themselves in supplying shops and supermarkets. Regulators may turn a blind eye to small-scale box schemes (Community-supported Agriculture) or backdoor sales to neighbours, particularly if they don't include items under stricter hygiene and safety controls, like eggs, dairy and meat products. Like most "blind eye" practices, however, it really comes down to the goodwill of neighbours, and as we've seen, they're not all on board the local food wagon. Particularly not if it brings increased traffic and noise or decreased air quality, or if the neighbours simply belong to the "rules are rules" school of thought.

But neither regulators nor cranky neighbours can object to urban farmers who are able to barter food for other goods or services with whomever they choose; and perhaps that is a route for some to explore. We'll come back to that when we talk about the future.

Apart from regulations affecting food production, shops and supermarkets have their own requirements, which will be obvious to you when you peruse the produce aisles. Note the regularity of the products, the careful washing and trimming, the standardized packaging and the labels and barcodes.

As a supplier, to enter this arena you need to accept a fairly low selling price to allow the store its profit margin. You have to provide food items that are standard in size, shape and quality, and are free of blemishes; deliver them regularly; and prepare to be dropped with no notice if the store's requirements or purchasing policies change. It's an unequal relationship, and so most small producers prefer, if they can, to sell at markets or by CSA or through farmgate methods, such as front-yard vegetable stands, that create a more equal and direct relationship between seller and buyer.

Farmgate sales are likely going to be prohibited in your neighbourhood, as municipalities do not want complaints about noise and traffic generated by your customers' coming and going. At a minimum, you'll need a display table, some kind of food packaging and a way to keep the food fresh and/or chilled. You'll also have to decide between manning the farm stand and relying on honesty boxes for payment. It's a sad reality that few urban neighbourhoods can expect honesty boxes to remain unpilfered. I've seen a couple of unmanned peri-urban farm stands that employ webcams to keep the customers honest, but the Big Brother route certainly isn't to every farmer's liking.

There are, of course, farmers' markets. The headline-grabbing figure of $3.09 billion in economic impact announced in the Farmers' Markets Canada 2008 study certainly caught the attention of municipal planners across the country. Later that year, the Farmers' Markets Association of Manitoba Co-op published its own study, which said the economic impact of farmers' markets in Manitoba alone was $10.26 million. The Alberta Farmers' Market Association reported $388 million for 2008, while Ontario estimated $641 million to $1.9 billion.

Though farmers' markets sound like a simple low-complexity approach to selling, in today's regulated world, it's not simple to set up enterprises of this kind in cities: it takes local government commitment, land and money to pull it off, as well as the force of will of people able to navigate both the interests of farmers and those of regulators and consumers. There are zoning and health regulations, liability and infrastructure concerns. Space, amenities and services need to be planned. Marketing and promotion are necessary. Selling spaces need to be large enough to set up displays, to allow access and power for mobile cooling units like freezers, and to be convenient for customers to get to. In most cases, the venue for the market will be in use only during part of the year, and that's a big issue for space planning in urban centres where land is costly and in demand year-round.

Many urban consumers are spoiled for choice in buying produce, so farmers' markets have a lot of work to do to prove that they are a real alternative to more usual convenience outlets like supermarkets. Largely seen as an option for affluent locavores, farmers' markets often fall short in serving the lower-income households that could most benefit from access to reasonably priced fresh produce – often the markets are awkwardly located for public transit users; often they attract niche sellers of higher priced products. In locations like Edmonton, Halifax, Toronto and Saskatoon, where the markets are operated year-round in covered spaces, they are more likely to be seen as a real alternative to supermarket shopping. This allows them to build a year-round customer base, which seasonal markets cannot do.

And seasonality, like so much to do with food security, is central to the concept of farmers' markets. Most of the country is not growing food year-round (our climate gets in the way), although Eliot Coleman and others who grow year-round in unheated greenhouses demonstrate a sustainable way to extend the growing season, and in urban heat islands this opportunity could be taken more often. The seasonal farmers' markets are geared to the spring-through-fall offerings of fresh fruit and vegetables. This has as much to do with the open-air settings of such markets as it does with the merchandise: neither can cope with Canadian winters.

But more can be done. Indoor winter markets could offer local meats, baked goods, storage produce like root vegetables and apples, and preserved and locally processed foods like cheese and canned fruits. Winter greens and sprouts, where available, fly off the tables on those dark chilly days. But supplying a market year-round will take adjustments on both sides: consumers will have to stay true to the food producers, and producers will have to plan for a year's worth of sales. It takes some rethinking of the agricultural working year, which has traditionally given farmers the winter off in compensation for the long working days governed by natural cycles of growth and harvest.

Variations on the farmers' market theme come and go. University students are often keen on sustainability, and so there are campus markets – McMaster in Hamilton started one last year; there's one at Waterloo and another at the University of Victoria. But the University of British Columbia, in Vancouver, has the edge on all of them. Unlike the others, which rely on student volunteers to sell local produce purchased from farms, UBC has a well-established farm and has been selling at its own Saturday market since 2001.

Pocket Markets and Buying Clubs

In Victoria, pocket markets – small urban markets set up in offices or other public spaces – were tried as a way of grouping farmers together to get their produce to a buying public. The markets were initially successful, but then several forces – including the success of efforts to get people growing their own produce – converged to sink them. I suspect another reason for the pocket markets' demise was the emergence of many new farmgates and farmers' markets that provided direct competition.

The pocket markets that had been set up in recreation centres didn't thrive because the buying public tended to come to the centres armed only with a fitness pass, ill-prepared for food shopping. Those in office buildings met problems with security: if they couldn't be held in post-security areas there wasn't always space for them, and office managers started clamping down on the e-mails that promoted the markets and the foods on offer.

But the idea of scaling down a farmers' market into a foyer-size urban space is attractive to a lot of consumers, and the obstacles are not insurmountable. The Pocket Market Toolkit, developed and shared online by Victoria organization FoodRoots (which originated the pocket market concept), has proved popular in Vancouver and the lower mainland of BC, where such markets are a going concern.

FoodRoots has turned its attention to small-scale distribution in several other ways, currently offering an organic/natural foods buying club, as well as workshops and outreach projects. Many other Canadian cities also have food co-operatives or buying clubs that allow consumers to bypass conventional retail and buy direct from sources that practice sustainable or ethical production, while getting the benefits of collective purchasing power.

Community-supported Agriculture (CSA)

CSA is perhaps the acronym for our time as so many people question the effects of a global market economy on our lives and look to smaller-scale, community-based alternatives. The principles can be applied and transformed in many ways. CSA programs originated in Switzerland and Japan in the 1960s and gained popularity in Europe before arriving in North America in the 1980s.

Although consumers may view a CSA as a food subscription – typically offering a season of weekly boxes of assorted fruit and vegetables, but with any number of variations, from honey to grain to meat – the scheme actually exists to share the financial risk of producing food. Farming is a precarious enterprise, subject to the oscillating costs of seeds, equipment and supplies. Farmers who invest money as well as time in food production are left holding the bag in times of drought, flood or market whim. With a guaranteed market and money up front, they can afford to plant and make a reasonable prediction about their yields and incomes. CSAs also allow farmers to take the whole profit rather than the share paid to them after middlemen and marketers and retailers have taken their cuts.

In return, consumers receive food of known quality. Being in a direct relationship with the food producer, they can learn exactly how the food has been grown. CSA farmers may deliver the boxes to their urban customers, or the customers may visit the farms or collect the wares at farmers' markets. CSAs requiring travel to the farm give the consumer the added benefit of actually seeing the fields where their food is grown.

In a very few programs, CSA subscribers are required, or at least encouraged, to take a physical hand in the growing and/or harvesting of their food. This is an important way to teach people to value their food, to feel fully connected to its source. Even a CSA relationship where the consumer comes to the farm to collect the weekly veg box is a retail relationship; it's like supermarket shopping – but better, of course – and it places the purchaser in a familiar and comfortable position. You are only a buyer, not a maker or a grower: unless you make the extra effort to find out more about how the food is produced, the setup can maintain that distance between eater and producer that allows us to be wasteful of our food and fickle in our support of local businesses.

CSA schemes are of particular relevance to urban agriculture because they can be scaled up or down as needed. Beginning farmers or those with little available land are often shut out of more lucrative sales outlets that require a constant quantity and quality of food products. With unpredictable weather on the one hand and a rise in interest in local eating on the other, CSAs have filled a necessary middle ground, permitting small farms to start up and remain afloat. CSAs have allowed urban farmers to tap a revenue source and feed their neighbours at the same time.

Self-sufficient Institutions

Public institutions are gradually bowing to public pressure and sourcing more local and seasonal produce, where available. Still, this is a difficult change for schools, hospitals and other institutions where budgets are under constant pressure. Locally grown food typically means fresh fruits, vegetables and meats, which need on-site storage and preparation. Preparation means staffing, and staffing means higher labour costs. Many institutional kitchens have adapted to budget cuts by bringing in more ready-made foods that need only be heated and served.

Public institutions are often locked into long-term service contracts with catering companies that – thanks to sophisticated logistical systems, global food contracts and economies of scale – can provide a full range of food at a fraction of the price of buying local ingredients. The use of these catering companies, however, locks public institutions into the vagaries of pricing that will be affected by global sourcing: global supplies that fluctuate in our uncertain weather and political climate, and the uncertainties of fuel supplies and fuel prices going forward. It can result in institutional food that is unpalatable in more than one way.

Unless they are willing to put food security above all other interests, our governments, whether municipal, provincial or federal, may find they have tied their own hands through trade agreements that prevent them from setting procurement policies favouring local producers. We need to make ourselves aware of the trade agreements our governments are party to on our behalf, and let our legislators know that food security must come first.

Restrictions are imposed by such agreements as the New West Partnership Trade Agreement (the free trade agreement between BC, Alberta and Saskatchewan that put an end to the Buy BC program); the current (at time of writing) Comprehensive Economic and Trade Agreement (CETA) talks between Canada and the European Union, which reach down into municipal procurement and put such initiatives as Toronto's food policy at risk; the Canada–US Trade Agreement (CUSTA), the North American Free Trade Agreement (NAFTA), and the General Agreement on Tariffs and Trade (GATT), with their direct and indirect hampering of local food policies; and the Harper government's ongoing moves to "harmonize" trade regulations with the US.

When you think about it, there is scope for a great many public and private institutions – daycare centres, schools, colleges, hospitals, care homes, prisons, young-offender and remand centres, group homes and government cafeterias – to implement some aspects of food production, or to integrate local food into their catering policies; but many of them will only make the change under pressure from their eating publics.

If food isn't worth making noise about, what is?

URBAN ANIMALS

Traffic in domesticated animals was recorded as long ago as 4000 BCE: "farm" animals have long lived among us, rural and urban, in a state of mutual dependence. It is only over the past couple of centuries that concerns over hygiene and the logistics of housing our bulging urban populations have led to the banishment of animals from our cities.

Some significant social problems have arisen from this. The most damaging is our utter dissociation from sources of meat. In sending our meat production out of town, we've abandoned our own role in safeguarding our food animals and making their lives productive as part of a whole food system. We've lost the sense of the "virtuous circle" in which we both produce food and eat it, which is the best way to guarantee that we'll not only value it but also ensure that it will be safe and nutritious.

By allowing our food to be produced without any concern except affordability, we've created the profit-driven corporations that race to reduce costs. The cold-heartedness of cost efficiencies and the steadfastly blind eye of the consumer have led us to factory farming, which keeps its operations well hidden from public view.

When any product is produced as cheaply as possible, quality declines. Quite apart from the sheer cruelty of factory farming, cheapening animal production destroys the quality of animals' lives, which in turn destroys the quality of the food products they ultimately become. Animals are deliberately bred in ways that deform them and cause them lifelong pain and suffering. In animal-based food products we now see declining nutritional quality and escalating incidences of food-borne and food-related illnesses – the hidden costs of cheap food, which will be borne by future generations.

Even today we have a generation (or more) of children with no connection to nature, a condition serious enough to warrant its own name and field of study: "nature-deficit disorder." It is crucial that these children start to learn about a nature that includes the domesticated food animals whose fortunes affect their own health and the future of their food supply. Many of these animals can be a welcome part of an urban agriculture system, even as other members of the animal kingdom are adapting to urban life alongside us and are unwelcome visitors in our nascent gardens.

Bees and Other Insects

Honeybees are excellent urban animals. Like most urban animals in North America, they are not native species but specialized livestock imported by settlers wanting the comforts of home. Like livestock, they need tending. Without care they may sicken and die, or get overcrowded to the point that they swarm and half the hive disappears. Keepers need to understand their illnesses, their cycles and their nutritional needs in all seasons, and, come harvest time, to find a way to extract the honey.

There is a gratifying surge of interest in beekeeping among urbanites, young and old. Hives are finding a place even on hotel rooftops – as in Vancouver and Toronto – and tucked away in gardens everywhere. Their food supply in suburban areas is assured, as long as flower gardens outnumber food gardens. But even food gardeners in cities can offer nourishment for bees by letting some crops go to flower, and by growing bee-friendly plants and providing a water supply – supplied with a landing rock – for them.

Access to food and water are not enough, however. Canadian beekeepers, rural and urban, have suffered tremendous hive losses in recent years, and it can be hard to know whom to believe when the causes are explored.

A recent study that purported to solve the riddle – blaming the bee losses on stress, fungal diseases and parasites rather than pesticides – turns out to have been led by someone with a vested interest in the pesticide industry. When biotech firms fund as much agricultural research as they do nowadays, it is hardly surprising to see the researchers dancing all too lightly around the possibility that bee deaths are caused by the pesticides those firms make. I have seen numerous articles postulating all kinds of theories about causes of hive losses, only to conclude with the advice that homeowners time their pesticide applications for times of day when honeybees are less active. Why are the writers emboldened to write this much, yet stop short of adding the obvious conclusion?

To any sane person, it beggars belief that pesticides – applied so liberally by so many, for everything from houseplants to mega-farms – should have nothing to do with the problem. Bees are insects, too, and chemical insecticides make little distinction between the kinds of insects they kill. Our gardens are depleted of friendly insects, including honeybees, thanks to these sprays and powders. And any chemical intervention, even a homemade one, is bound to inflict "collateral damage."

Even if honeybees are not killed immediately by insecticides on their food plants, they can poison their community by bringing contaminated pollen and nectar to the hive – and that toxic nectar may well become honey consumed by humans.

There are certainly other factors besides pesticides contributing to hive losses. The fungal condition nosema and the varroa mite are taking their toll in weakening an embattled insect, and both are thought to be developing resistance to the standard treatments.

But honeybees are not the only pollinators in urban farms and gardens. Bumblebees are another pollinator we can cultivate in cities: there are some 250 species of them worldwide, about 50 of which are in North America, but their numbers are threatened by the usual culprits of habitat loss and pesticide use. Some diseases particular to bumblebees are transmitted by imported foreigners brought into new territories by commercial greenhouse operations; in the well-worn tradition of human interference, some of these bees inevitably escape and wreak havoc in their new and alien ecosystem. Homeowners can build bee boxes to encourage bumblebees, but otherwise the bees need un-disturbed ground or trees for nests.

In some areas, up to 70 per cent of wild bee species are ground-dwellers, living under rocks or in rotted logs, so such materials are essential for the urban garden. Our aesthetic ideal for gardens is not necessarily shared by the real animals and insects who need to live there.

In the orchards of the lower mainland and Vancouver Island, the blue orchard bee (*Osmia lignaria*) – a kind of mason bee – emerges ear-lier in the spring than the honeybee, in time for the fruit blossoms. Gardeners can nurture and encourage blue orchard bees by creat-ing habitats, including bee boxes, which are popular in many backyards. Like many wild pollinators, these bees don't have the range of honeybees, so habitats need to be placed close to home, within five hundred metres of fruit trees.

Other pollinators might look like flies or wasps; they perform the same valuable func-tion as the honeybee. Understanding how they live and what they eat, year-round, allows gardeners to encourage these pollinators. Bee-friendly gardens attract far more than just honeybees.

There are of course destructive insects, and through overuse and lack of imaginative alternatives, our chemical weapons are losing power against those. Growing concerns about the harmful effects of pesticides – contaminating the fruits of food plants, killing beneficial insects, sickening people and pets, and leaching into the water supply – seem finally to be leading toward a nationwide stiffening of pesticide regulations, against the powerful vested interests of chemical companies and over the wailing of gardeners who have come to depend on them.

The fight may not be over, but so far Dow AgroSciences has not yet won its lawsuits that claim provincial pesticide bans in Ontario and Quebec violate terms of the North American Free Trade Agreement. In a happy moment in 2010, a similar claim by Chemtura, which asked the Canadian government to compensate it for losses arising out of provincial bans on cosmetic lawn pesticides, was thrown out by NAFTA arbitrators, who also saw fit to charge Chemtura with Canada's legal costs in defending the claim.

While the corporate machines grind through the legal heights, we on the ground are reminded daily that urban spaces are adjoining spaces, so you are only as environmentally friendly as your neighbours. If your neighbour decides to spray his crops with pesticides, these can be carried on the air to you, or find their way into your soil and plants through groundwater. Conversely, if your neighbour uses humane methods of disposing of snails or slugs, you might end up with a garden full of refugees. All these factors are magnified when we share community growing spaces.

We are fortunate, in urban gardens, to be working on a scale small enough to allow such labour-intensive pest management methods as hand-picking. This is not everyone's idea of a good time or perfect solution: the thousands of slugs I drowned in my soapy bucket last year were seemingly replaced by legions more.

Clearly we need to seek allies in nature to keep our gardens producing for us rather than becoming cafeterias for unwelcome opportunists.

Integrated pest management (IPM) is the name given to a number of different but complementary techniques to control pests while minimizing the use of pesticides. Our native species of ladybugs (lady beetles) – including their imported and outnumbering cousins the Asian lady beetles – are among the most common biological agents used in gardens and greenhouses, due to their voracious appetite for aphids. Immortalized on greeting cards, in nursery rhymes and as endearing cartoon characters, these colourful carnivores can consume a thousand aphids a day, their hungry offspring about four hundred.

Shocking but true: few urbanites would recognize the ladybug larva. Long and spiky, the bristly dragon-like adolescent is an even better hunter than its adult counterpart. How many of these have died at the hands of panicking amateur gardeners we will never know, but we need someone to make a sympathetic cartoon idol of the juvenile if we are to assure the future of the adult.

Chickens

The next most numerous domestic animal is ideally suited for life in the city. It needs relatively little living space, eats kitchen scraps and garden pests, and helps to fertilize the garden. It will give you an egg a day for quite a long time and, when it stops laying, can be converted to a familiar protein source. Plus: it's got character, likes to be petted and can be very pretty. What's not to like?

Just as our egalitarian society has evolved to the point where we don't do master-servant relationships easily, our Disneyfied relationship with animals has detached us from the farmer-animal stance. We may enter into chicken ownership unprepared for the time, equipment, costs and decisions involved in keeping them.

The chicken is the only food animal many urbanites would consider getting, and that interest is focused on the eggs. The difficulties begin when a chicken ails – many of its special-ized ailments and susceptibilities are beyond the ken of city folk to diagnose or home remedy – and when it stops laying.

Chickens do stop laying during the year, part of a natural cycle that is tortured out of commercial layers to keep them producing year-round, through tricks with lighting. But they also stop laying after several years – three, in most cases, although chickens can live for up to 14 years. That's a big gap. Some urban chicken-keepers feel that old hens are worth keeping on because of their charm and their value in pest control and food-into-fertilizer transformation. But others may not have thought through the ethics of what to do after the laying period. If you're keeping chickens for food security reasons, it's a cold hard question: can you afford to go on paying another 11 years of animal feed and upkeep for a non-laying hen?

Three years is long enough for your hen to get a name, a character and a place in the family. And that's just the point when the ruthless farmer in you may have to kick in and wring old Henrietta's neck ... only you're not allowed to do that. So you must pack her into the family sedan – perhaps her only ride, so she'll be very upset and squawk the whole way – and take her to a slaughterhouse, where they'll treat her like, well, any old bird. Distressing on both sides.

As if that were not enough, you must be guard and protector to your animals. Once you have hens, you discover, you must be home by dusk every day so long as you both shall live, because if the hens are not tucked up in bed and the lock securely placed, you'll have trouble with anything from rats to raccoons. During the day you'll need to protect them from birds of prey – owls, eagles, hawks – as well as cats and dogs, not to mention human carelessness with the latch to the pen, which can cost you a bird and/or as many vegetables as it can consume during a breakout. If you're in a part of Canada that gets very cold in the winter, you'll need to winterize the hen house and keep the chickens warm.

And then you have to keep them healthy. Not all urban farmers will have access to a veterinarian who's up to speed on avian ailments – the particular lice, parasites and infections they're prone to. It takes time for support systems to catch up with any trend, and animal trends are no exception. While the needs of cats and dogs are well catered for by urban vets, there has not been so much call for city chicken doctors until recently. The conditions faced by urban hens may differ somewhat from those in rural set-ups as well: in larger chicken operations, hens are often simply not treated because it's cheaper to dispose of them. Urbanites accustomed to spending three- or four-figure sums keeping family pets alive will have to decide whether equal treatment applies to the hen house.

If you do find a vet, you again have ethical choices to make if you decide to keep your hens beyond the laying stage. Because of selective breeding that makes them good layers, older hens are vulnerable to reproductive cancers and associated illnesses, as well as the compounding ailments of old age. Veterinary and other costs can quickly exceed the estimated three hundred dollars per year that owners spend on each healthy bird.

You will of course not have a rooster, because those create noise ... as well as offspring. So when the time comes to add replacement hens, you'll have to buy more female chicks and raise those with due care. When you pick up your new flock of beauties, spare a thought for their male siblings, who are surplus to human requirements and so may have met a sordid end – not all are disposed of in humane ways.

You'll have to learn about chicken psychology and the source of the expression "pecking order." Sometimes, a chicken farmer told me, you just get a mean bunch and they kill one another. This may be a rare occurrence in a small backyard flock. But the fact is that these are animals with agendas other than looking ornamental and laying your breakfast.

Other Urban Animals

Some urban farmers keep rabbits as a source of manure and as meat animals; but again you're going to have to be prepared to weigh the cost of feed and care against the value of the rabbit output. In other gardens, rabbits dig and dine at random and are simple pests. They could be supper if we were able to trap them, perhaps. But like many urban animals, they are a problem without a predator.

Bambi is at best a garden vandal: the urban deer is the bane of the urban grower. Voracious, nimble and beautiful, deer are almost impossible to deal with in today's city, where their predators are mainly automobiles, although their presence also attracts cougars from time to time.

Until we find a way to integrate urban deer into our food supply, or otherwise control their numbers, urban animal lovers will carry on feeding them and protesting deer culls. This puts the onus on city-dwellers to deer-proof their gardens with acres of not inexpensive deer fence and garden covers, or give up growing altogether.

Birds – which, let's remember, include songbirds and hummingbirds but also crows, ravens, seagulls and Canada geese – raise a variety of issues. Small birds are invaluable helpers for picking grubs, worms and caterpillars out of our garden beds and fruit trees, and even take a hand in pollination, but they also share our tastes for certain urban crops. They can strip a tree of cherries, ruin a plum or apple crop by sampling the wares or devastate a freshly seeded garden. In my neighbourhood the sparrows have developed a selective taste for chard, and they strip young leaves down to the stems. Netting can help, but many a robin has been found tangled in my neighbour's blueberry net.

Crows and ravens can uproot a crop of seedlings if they think something tasty is living in the soil: I saw one farmer's field denuded by ravens who were hunting wireworm, and more than once they've scattered the content of my front door planters while looking for lunch. They are strong and smart enough to toss a bit of row cover away if that's all that lies between them and their next meal.

Geese are seldom a problem in smaller yards since they prefer wide-open spaces, but it's conceivable, given slim pickings elsewhere, or a soft-headed neighbour feeding them, that they will take a fancy to garden greens or urban grain crops. Their size and number make them formidable eaters.

And then there are raccoons, one of the most common and complex urban animals. They love a lot of tree fruits and have been found to be fond of corn and other foods. But as long as they can find other food sources, are generally not too great a threat to the crops on an urban farm.

The real problem with raccoons is faced by urban chicken-keepers. Raccoons love eggs and will kill chickens and rabbits if they can get at them. They're not too hard to keep out of a chicken coop, but much harder to keep out of the garden, particularly if you are blessed with animal-loving neighbours who feed them or have easy-open garbage bins.

In most cities of the world, people coexist with rats. Unless reinforced with brick and hardware cloth, our compost bins feed them; rats may also develop a taste for random food crops or your carefully harvested seed selection in the garden shed. Fruit tree grower Bob Duncan, on the Saanich Peninsula in BC, reports that they enjoy nibbling on lemon skins and apples.

Their tree-dwelling relatives, grey squirrels, are fond of nut crops and do not distinguish between stash locations, burying in – and then digging to retrieve from – lawns, gardens and flowerpots. Local authorities in my neighbourhood consider them an invasive pest and order them done away with if captured.

Cities have grown so quickly that they've infringed on habitat of all kinds. Few of us might think of bears as a garden pest, but those in the suburbs and peri-urban areas of large cities, or in smaller urban centres certainly need to consider them. Lacking sufficient food or wilderness, they pilfer urban fruit trees, beehives and gardens. Other animals formerly found only in the wild – coyotes, for example – are making incursions into our cities and keeping the urban ecosystems in flux.

Fish

Urban farmers can and do incorporate aquatic

species into their repertoire. Will Allen, the founder of Milwaukee-based Growing Power, an educational urban farming organization, has inspired many to try growing tilapia and yellow perch as part of an integrated and self-sustaining food system.

Tilapia are plant-eaters by nature, feeding on aquatic matter like duckweed and algae; they are ideal city fish because they can be reared in relatively crowded environments, like barrels. Their excrement is a valuable fertilizing agent for land and aquatic plants; the aquatic plants help to filter contamination from the water; the trimmings from fish provide excellent compost for land-based plantings; and so the cycle continues. Other species can be added to an aquaculture setup, such as fresh-water prawns that feed on fish waste, and an artificial stream can be set up to run through a greenhouse system.

Small-scale aquaculture is a better source of tilapia than supermarkets, because the ones found in stores are increasingly raised in Asian fish farms and treated like the rest of our industrial livestock: fed on grain and dosed with antibiotics, antifungals and antibacterials like formalin (formaldehyde).

Waste

All the urban animals we've been talking about bring with them a host of challenges, but they also bring benefits, notably animal waste – manure – a byproduct that has always been hugely important to both traditional farming and backyard gardening.

The biggest issue we as a planet have to face in growing our own food is that of replenishing the soil. We're losing, some say, 1 per cent of global topsoil per year. We've been able to wipe out in decades what has taken millennia to build up. Too much of what we haven't lost, we've built on, paved over, contaminated or otherwise abused to the point of infertility. Chemical fertilizers are known to deplete the soil's natural fertility, and uneven management practices in city and country alike put our ability to feed the world at risk. That's a lot of wasted damaged earth.

The good news is, it is possible – indeed

essential – to build soil fertility by composting. Some of us do this already; a few far-sighted municipalities have already addressed it with public composting collections. If every household in every part of the country stopped throwing compostables away, we could have a spectacular result and a real crack at creating a viable food supply in cities. But it takes persistence, commitment and a clear understanding of the materials and the methods – not a hopeful combination for the disposable generation. Squeamishness, apathy and trouble with rats put a lot of urbanites off; so do sheer ignorance and a hectic lifestyle. Too many city-dwellers embrace the idea but cannot find the time to manage it; their compost languishes and their worms die. So it will take regulation and enforcement to bring about lasting change.

A full-scale composting program means more than leaves and a few vegetable parings: it means food scraps of all kinds – meat, bones, cheese rinds – as well as waste paper, cardboard, hair, natural fabrics and clothing, tea bags, coffee grounds and much more besides.

It means using different methods for different foodstuffs – compost bins, vermiculture, digesters and aerobic and anaerobic methods all have their place. As it breaks down, compost generates heat that kills pathogens in the raw materials, and this can be used – as market gardeners in 18th-century Paris, and many since, demonstrated with their use of hotbeds – to heat the soil and keep off-season plants growing through the winter.

Will Allen heats some of the Growing Power greenhouses with heaps of compost. He likes to say he's in direct competition with the municipal garbage trucks for control of local food waste, and his work with worms and large-scale composting pays off by the ton in food produced by urban farms he's helped to start. He can convert truckloads of unsold produce, together with the cartons it comes in, into useable compost in eight to 12 months: the work goes on, even through a Wisconsin winter. He feeds the compost to worms that eat their weight in food each day; worm castings are fabulously nutritious for the soil, and they profit his enterprise when he sells them to the public.

Backyard chickens and other animals produce a manageable amount of manure that can be used to benefit a backyard farm or garden. Factory farms do not. Such is the scale of intensive animal production that its waste products are no longer a boon to the earth but a contaminant of earth, water and air. In his book *Eating Animals*, Jonathan Safran Foer cites USDA figures quantifying the manure produced annually by pig farms (7.2 million pounds), broiler chicken barns (6.6 million pounds) and cattle feedlots (344 million pounds). And that's before you factor in the quantities of antibiotics and hormones and other chemicals that are excreted in all that. Canadian figures will be lower, but we do buy American meat, as well, so we're responsible for some of their waste, too.

There is one other animal whose waste products directly affect the urban landscape, and that is humans. China was famed for centuries for its careful use of "night soil" to enrich its fields. But now that it's modernized, it's joining the rest of the developed world in channelling human and other municipal waste products into sewage, one of the biggest municipal headaches of our time.

The problem is that sewage combines industrial with bodily waste and excreted pharmaceuticals, and the product is potentially toxic, laced with heavy metals and chemical fire retardants even after treatment or large-scale composting. The resulting sludge, if it's not pumped into oceans or rivers, is provided free to farmers by municipalities that don't know what else to do with it. Most people don't realize how much of the conventional produce we buy from supermarkets was grown in sewage sludge, and that chemicals like chemical fire retardants can be transmitted through plant material grown in soils contaminated with them. (Sludge is not allowed in organic growing.)

Ironically, just as grave concerns are surfacing about the looming shortages of our other key non-renewable resource, phosphorus, I read that human waste is now the largest single source of phosphorus emerging from cities. Straight human urine, freshly dispensed and diluted by 10, makes an excellent source of nitrogen, potassium and phosphorus for compost or garden. And "humanure" (the composting version of human waste), produced with a composting toilet, is a real and available option that would allow us to compost human waste instead of mixing it with toxins and then sharing it with the natural world in quantities nature can't cope with.

While we're talking about what we're flushing down the drain, we need to think about another endangered resource: water. Agriculture accounts for some 70 per cent of water use worldwide and is considered particularly inefficient, returning only about 25 per cent of water consumed to its water table. This is because most of the water goes into irrigation (with losses from runoff and evaporation), and livestock watering and processing. A lot of water is removed from the land in the form of food products like vegetables that are not routinely returned to it in liquid form. What water does find its way back into our aquifers and other water sources may be loaded with nitrates, pharmaceuticals, pesticides and bacteria, as well as other pathogens from large-scale agriculture.

A sustainable agriculture, whether urban or rural, is one that conserves water and makes it part of the agricultural cycle. Water issues soon come to the fore for urban farmers, who may be using growing spaces they do not own: they may have to negotiate use of someone else's tap and drainage systems, and consider how water harvesting might figure in the picture.

Cities, with their vast impermeable surface area, are at particular risk because they disrupt water's cycling between earth and sky. Stormwater runoff across roofs, roads and parking lots diverts into storm drains, sewage systems and directly into streams, rivers and oceans bearing its load of garbage and surface contaminants, instead of filtering through soil and vegetation to replenish our water table.

Grey water (water from washing machines, sinks and showers) and rainwater diverted into barrels or cisterns are two additional sources of water for use in urban gardens. Although grey water has long been used by more frugal nations, Canadian municipalities have been slow to encourage its use, which remains illegal in many parts of the country, the chief concern being that the pipes may back up into freshwater supplies.

There are concerns about the use of rainwater in food gardens, where it has been collected from downspouts. The most common roofing surface used on Canadian homes is asphalt, which can leach petroleum into the water, and then into food gardens. Wooden roofing shingles may have been treated with chemical preservatives that also contaminate the rainwater; cedar is too acidic for use on plants. Some metal roofs, particularly older ones, contain and leach heavy metals or moss inhibitors. So it seems the safest roof coverings from which to harvest water for food gardens are, because of climate or cost, the least used on Canadian homes: slate, glazed tile and fibreglass.

THE FUTURE OF
URBAN AGRICULTURE

In the past decade, there has been a lot of interest in the media and elsewhere in urban agriculture, even though, as we have seen, it is hardly a new concept. Cities in the developing world have made an art of eking food out of impossible spaces, and we can learn much from them.

I believe the future of food-secure cities – and food production in general – lies in diversification and localization. Instead of putting all our eggs into one agri-basket, we must produce more foods from within the cities themselves, so we're less reliant on transported goods for basic sustenance. This also makes us less reliant on a handful of crops for our food staples: small-scale production in our own backyards frees us from the restrictions imposed by monocultures. Home gardeners can grow anything we like – and grow for flavour and nutrition – since our own crops need not be geared to the convenience of mechanical harvesting or the rigours of long-haul transport.

But reinventing urban agriculture in our modern world – with its snarls of health regulations and land-use zonings, its vandals and vermin, its addiction to machines and pesticides, its contaminated brownfield sites and endangered water supplies – is not going to be easy. Nor is it necessarily going to be sustainable. Humans have proven throughout history to be a short-sighted and self-interested species, fickle in their interests, and the urban specimen is accustomed neither to sharing nor to planning for an uncertain future.

Necessity (through hunger) is a powerful motivator, but food takes time to grow, and more important so do the food networks we may urgently need long before all of us are ready. We will require a variety of approaches, and time to develop and refine enough growing methods to keep as wide a population as possible engaged and motivated in finding new ways to grow food.

At the rate of change we're seeing today, any revolutionary new solutions I could name will – I hope – be outdated within a few years. All I can offer here are some hopes for the future and discussion of what seem to me to be useful directions we could take. Many of these will not be considered new by back-to-the-landers, contemporary agripreneurs or even longtime readers of *Mother Earth News* and *Harrowsmith*, but they are changes I believe we need to make in order to assure urban food security in Canada.

If we are to feed ourselves and our mushrooming urban populations through the centuries to come, urban agriculture will need to become commonplace, part of our mental landscape. This is a global, no-end-in-sight Victory Garden project that needs a global, community and individual commitment to protect and nurture our agricultural land, and to produce food in every precious space we have.

It seems obvious that we can't rely on our governments – municipal, provincial or federal – to act with the speed and impartiality our need for food security will require. Our shattered sense of community needs to be rebuilt, for, as the saying goes, there can be no food security if your neighbour is hungry.

For starters, we have no choice but to learn how to cook again. If we are to control our future, we need to start with what goes into our bodies, and our children's. We need to learn those skills of growing, harvesting and preserving. Throw away the plastic bottles of condiments and make our own, giving ourselves back the power to say how much sugar, fat and salt we want. We should be preparing for a less well-equipped future: we must assume a mantle of survivalism and learn how to make do; how to forage and dry herbs and hand-mix bread dough. We need to seek out missing knowledge from elders, friends and neighbours, and teach the next generation the skills that will make them truly self-sufficient in an uncertain world.

We should all learn to grow at least some of our own food in less than perfect spaces and conditions. Whether we pick up large or small farming tools is a matter of choice and opportunity, but we'll need to pick up something. We can start by sharing the seeds of knowledge – and their fruits – with our neighbours.

Urban agriculture can create meaningful jobs. Increasing numbers of people in our cities are farming in backyards, peri-urban farms and improvised growing spaces; raising hens or keeping bees; foraging for mushrooms, nuts, berries or seaweed; and doing so for the pleasure of producing food that they can sell. They are teaching others to do this, through work parties, workshops or apprenticeship programs. Small-scale food processing is also on the rise: baking, jam, teas, spice mixes, cheese and meat products are being sold in small quantities at markets or in CSA programs. These producers may not be making much income, but they are eating well and creating an employment niche that must surely bring vastly more pleasure and self-respect than would an eight-hour shift at a call centre.

For years we've been hearing that people won't choose farming because it's hard work. But for anyone who's worked an office job, unpaid through lunch hours and evenings; who's been undermined by colleagues or bullied by employers; who's been reassigned, re-engineered or redeployed out of the job they thought they'd been hired for – is the physical toil of weeding rows of vegetables that you and your neighbours will eat really so difficult?

But it's not the hard graft that's at the heart of the problem. It's the lack of value – monetary and cultural – assigned to the job of growing food that keeps people off the farms. It has taken centuries of hand-me-down knowledge to teach the skills it takes to grow food well and keep agricultural land fertile. Farming, whether urban or rural, is a complex, life-giving profession that's been treated as disposable manual labour, its operations bastardized by chemicals and machines instead of managed by knowledgeable adaptable humans. That devaluing perception needs to change first, so that we have an experienced generation of farmers on hand to lead and teach us to survive in a food-insecure future.

Sustainability. The very word is as exhausted as our topsoil, after relatively short exposure as a buzzword. But self-sufficient, closed, agricultural loops are crucial to any vision of the future, whether in city or country. Visionaries who propose grand architectural solutions to food security are simply perpetuating the status quo and ignoring the realities of the situation. Proposing buildings that require vast quantities of steel – a raw material that requires energy-intensive mining and processing at a time when that energy is still powered only by fossil fuels – will never even enter the sustainability discussion.

To my mind, the best value-for-money solutions are those that attend to the connectedness of all life, that create a circularity of growing cycles and reduce the need for external inputs. That are low-technology and can endure through times when fossil-fuel energy is scarce or prohibitively expensive. That build on human interaction and co-operation, and self-sustain by allowing essential skills and knowledge to be endlessly shared and regenerated. That can be adapted to all shapes and sizes of growing spaces in city and country alike.

A lot of great ideas come out of Australia, particularly those to do with ways of growing food in drought-prone countries. On our drought-prone planet, we need all the ideas we can get to conserve and coax maximum use from water for food production. Permaculture is one of these, and it holds good possibilities for urban agriculture. Better still, its vision of sustainability includes the sharing of knowledge and the building of networks of knowledge, rather than the cultivation of a mere handful of experts.

It could be argued that permaculture is hardly futuristic, since it's been around for over 30 years, but it's neither well known nor widely practiced on commercial, let alone family, farms in Canada. As pressure grows on our water supplies and agricultural inputs rise in costs of many kinds, permaculture certainly deserves more attention as a way to design both urban and rural farms and gardens.

The principles of permaculture pay close attention to nature's methods of managing its soil, water and plants. Permaculturalists aim for gardens that are low maintenance, minimizing interventions like tillage that could erode the soil and disrupt its microorganisms, nutrients and drainage. The growing area is moulded in ways that incorporate water retention into its natural landscape and encourage plant growth and water conservation, harvesting and renewal.

One practice that incorporates permaculture design is forest gardening. This creates low-maintenance, perennial, food gardens, planted in vertical and mutually beneficial arrangements: trees (canopy layer), tall and short bushes, ground cover and vines. In order to repair the damage done to our climate and ecosystems from deforestation, we need to plant a lot of trees. They can serve a number of purposes: providing fruit, nuts or shade; using their deep roots to bring minerals to the surface and their leaves to replenish and protect the soil. Fruit trees need not be so large as to block light from neighbouring gardens or other parts of a backyard garden: the principle can be scaled to the space, light and topography available.

Another knowledge-sharing organism is rooting itself in Canada. The Transition Network started in England and has spread around the world as a community-powered response to peak oil and climate change. There were 63 Transition Initiatives in Canada at the time of writing.

The founders of the movement believe that peak oil – the moment when the amount of oil available is eclipsed by the demand for it – has already come. It makes little difference whether you believe that, or choose to believe the moment has yet to come – either way, there's no disputing it's an inevitable moment, and one that 21st-century civilization is not prepared for. Cheap oil is a temporary tool. Its loss is inevitable and its repercussions will be felt in every aspect of life, for it represents the loss of Western civilization's army of slaves (it's been estimated that one hundred slaves would be needed to do the work powered by one gallon of fossil fuel).

Unlike governments, Transition Initiatives put food security issues at the top of their list of concerns. They encourage communities to organize themselves in ways that restore communication and trust within urban centres. From such foundations, communities can improve their own food supplies by teaching one another – "re-skilling" – lost or innovative food production skills and developing alternative methods of trade and distribution. In some towns, local currencies allow food to be bartered for services or skills.

Barter is hardly new, of course: throughout agricultural history, barns have been raised in exchange for communal meals and returns of shared labour. In recent years, the goodwill of urban neighbours has been purchased for a few fresh eggs or a jar of honey, while residents wait for bylaws to catch up with the chickens or bees. Perhaps the loan of a garden tool or helping hand is worth a jar of jam or a few seedlings. A lesson in home preserving might be exchanged for one in building a compost system. And there are now "food swap" parties taking place in many cities, where people trade one handmade food item for another, meeting their neighbours in the process.

Bartering can range from a casual hand-to-hand exchange, to something much more formalized. Either way, you get to know your neighbours and you have a say in the value assigned to what you have and what you need.

Weaning populations from the seafood we're currently fishing to extinction in our oceans might be easier if local options were better explored on land. There are creative solutions being implemented in cities already – many of them thanks to the inspiration of Will Allen, whose Milwaukee Growing Power project proved how readily urban aquaculture could be included in an agricultural program.

For some years, Allen has been growing tilapia and perch use interlocking biosystems. Fish fertilize aquatic plants, which filter the fish waste and nurture water-borne organisms that also feed the fish, and round and round it goes. The FARM:shop project, which I visited in London, England, in late 2010, was clearly influenced by Allen's work. It proposed giving the fish a protein boost with soldier fly larvae, raised in the farm's compost, and adding freshwater prawns into its cycle, as they also feed on fish waste.

As for food waste, does it really need to be said? We have to stop throwing food and all other compostables into landfills. Edible and nutritious food that is not sold or needed by supermarkets should not be dumped with its non-biodegradable packaging into dumpsters but instead should be redistributed to food charities or for animal feed, or composted, or turned into fuel. Consumers are paying for the high degree of waste in our food stores, restaurants and processing plants – directly through the cost of the food we buy from them, and indirectly in the waste they produce. Every town and city in the country should be introducing mandatory composting programs and distributing the compost to urban growers.

Cities should be rethinking their approaches

to water and sewage, as well. Water needs to be conserved and mandatory grey water use introduced into all new building codes.

Sustainable cities visionary Herbert Girardet believes that waste water needs to be part of a closed soil-nutrient loop, so that we return the nitrogen and phosphorus from human waste back into food production. At the very least, composting toilets should be not only permitted but subsidized and promoted.

Before they seat themselves on their thrones, however, consumers need to understand what toxins they are contributing to the compost of the future by taking hormones and other medications. We need the political will to insist on accountability by the pharmaceutical industry when developing drugs that have a toxic effect on any part of our ecosystem, for we are all part of a food chain whose links are damaged by our failure to act as neighbours and equal citizens of our shared planet.

In all our cities, gleaning programs that pick and process unharvested tree fruit or nuts should be mandated to step in where tree owners don't. Community gleaning programs can and do share surplus fruit and either sell or process the rest as a matter of course, but they do not exist in every city, and participation by tree-owners is optional.

Gleaners should be mobilized to harvest "ugly" and unsaleable foods from farms for use in food production. Our learned addiction to uniformity – driven by the food-packaging and retail industry – and superficial perfection in our produce has certainly helped to create the situation where farmers cannot sell a curved cucumber, a lopsided apple or a two-legged carrot, regardless of flavour or nutritional value.

The land to grow that carrot will continue to be difficult to find on a crowded and expensive planet. How do we get around the need for land we can both grow and live on? I think Canadians need to start by taking responsibility for the size of the spaces they build. Our right to live in any-sized house is not, actually, god-given; it is the prerogative of a selfish culture that hasn't had to give the needs of all its members equal consideration. I cannot see how we can continue to allow retiring couples to build 370-square-metre dream homes and swimming pools on land fit for growing food.

When city planners review development permits, they need to attend to the solar rights of urban growers. Where land for urban food growing exists, or can be used, it needs to be protected from the development of multi-storey buildings that render adjoining spaces too dark and wind-whipped to be arable. Similarly, action needs to be taken against irresponsible urban plantings of oversized trees in back yards, such as sequoia or plane, and towering ornamentals like leyland cypress. In England whole municipal departments exist to deal with complaints about leylandii that have, unpruned, grown to their full 40-metre height, draining water, blocking light and sending roots into adjoining gardens.

But of course these are the ills of a dysfunctional culture: where neighbours are not preoccupied with walling off their neighbours, there is no need for oversized plantings. Community-building is the most important construct of any successful future: we need to find ways to tear home-owners away from their wired lives and electronic entertainments and get them outside where they can learn to be entertained by conversing and sharing food with the live human counterparts next door.

Where our cities are built on agricultural land, the problem is literally rooted in concrete. So many years of lax regulations and failures in environmental and agricultural safeguards have left us with a toxic legacy. Like SOLEfood, which transformed an East Vancouver parking lot into agricultural employment for homeless people, we can grow food on concrete if we must, as long as we can also grow compost to nourish that hard surface.

Beneath the paved surfaces, urban topsoil is mostly gone – trucked away during con-struction, contaminated by leaked or leaching toxins, or compressed beyond use. We need to pay attention to conserving and restoring what remains of bare soil as a matter of urgency, both urban and rural, and to ensure that dumping of building rubble is not permitted on any land fit for agricultural use.

Brownfield sites as well as public parks and golf courses will be top of the list when it comes time to commandeer land for growing – a process which, given public reluctance to address the food security problem voluntarily, will have to be driven by crisis, just as it was in Cuba. We need to develop the skills to deal with these different kinds of growing areas, and we should be working on their soil remediation and replenishment now.

Apartment-dwellers and those with mobility problems need not be excluded from the food-producing future. Windows can provide natural light to indoor pots or provide the foundation for window boxes or other growing structures; balconies can hold pots, vines and even mini-greenhouses. The smallest contribution – a pot of basil, a window box of carrots or lettuce – can cheer the view and involve you in your food. And for those with no space at all, there are community gardens; and if there are not, we need to demand that they be made available to all.

Because of their dependence on plastic, steel and fossil fuels, I cannot believe in shiny futuristic solutions to long-term food security, but they often make headlines in ways that more practical solutions never will. Some of the up-and-coming ideas are already underway. Others remain at the theoretical level, awaiting inspiration, investment and mobilization to test their mettle.

An idea floated by Dickson Despommier is that of growing a city's food in a kind of high-rise greenhouse. He has talked the idea up and been much quoted, but the first vertical farm has yet to be built. Grassroots it's not; it's a full-on city building project involving excavation, foundation and tonnes of glass and steel.

A similar but different idea from Swedish-American architects Plantagon proposes a new method of organic growing using a geodesic dome as a greenhouse; the dome can sit atop a highrise or operate as a stand-alone structure. Although that has yet to be built, at the time of writing, Plantagon has just started work on a vertical greenhouse in Linköping, Sweden.

If you don't like round, you can have diagonal, with another proposal from New York architects WORKac that resulted in a temporary urban farm and social space called P.F.1 (Public Farm 1), or the Harvest Green Project, which includes housing for farm workers, growing space and a farmers' market, and won a design competition in Vancouver in 2009.

Conclusion

Just as we've been trained not to know where our food comes from, we can learn to believe that urban agriculture can build community, green our urban spaces and improve food distribution in our cities.

One thing is certain: whatever does or doesn't get done by our governments and leaders, we individual citizens always have choices. And as long as we have them, we can make our views known by acting on them.

Vote with your fork, your pen, your shovel and your consumer dollar, for starters. But if you want to feed the future – your own, your neighbours' and your children's – you're going to have to learn how to produce food yourself and share that knowledge, and food, with your community.

URBAN AGRICULTURE GLOSSARY

100-mile Diet is a term, like **Locavore**, that refers to local seasonal eating. It's taken from the title of the 2007 book by Alisa Smith and J.B. MacKinnon and denotes the arbitrary distance within which all the food they consumed for a year must be grown.

Allotment Gardens allow individuals to grow food in an allocated space (often managed by and/or rented from a community or municipal organization). The term is sometimes used interchangeably with **Community Gardens**.

Aquaculture, or fish farming, can be introduced into cities: such species as tilapia, yellow perch and freshwater prawns raised in tanks can be part of a water-based food system.

Boulevards are city-owned common areas where food could potentially be grown. **Guerilla Gardeners** often target these areas for plantings. They may be located in areas of high vehicle traffic, and crops may be subject to dust and potential contamination by fuel exhaust or previous uses, as in the case of former gas stations.

Brownfield Sites are disused industrial sites within cities. Although they may offer enough acreage for community gardens and other urban farming initiatives, the soil may be poor in nutrients or structure, or contaminated by industrial chemicals, heavy metals and other toxins.

Buffer Zones in urban agriculture are areas that separate an agricultural business from its residential neighbours. These are crucial for preserving habitat for **Pollinators** and the rest of the ecosystem, for providing buffer space for agricultural smells and noises that might not be so attractive to neighbours, and for keeping agricultural lands safe from intrusion.

Chef Gardens are typically container or rooftop gardens in, on or next to restaurants; they enable the restaurants to grow herbs, greens or other ingredients on-site.

Co-disposal refers to the mingling of different kinds of waste in municipal waste management. This means that toxic and organic wastes are combined so that they cannot be safely composted for use in food-growing.

Commons is a term sometimes used in urban agriculture projects, where public land is used for community food-growing.

Community Gardens may refer to gardens that are run by public or community organizations, or those that are jointly tended by a group or committee. The purpose may be to raise food for the community or to bring a community together to raise food for donation. The term is sometimes used interchangeably with **Allotment Gardens**.

Community-supported Agriculture (CSA) is also known as "Community-shared Agriculture" or "box schemes." Subscribers pay farmers in advance and regularly receive a box of food. Usually CSA provides fruit or vegetables, but it is expanding into grain, honey, meats and even bread and baked goods.

Container Gardening can take place in anything filled with dirt, from plant pots to wading pools to burlap bags or ice-cream pails. It opens possibilities for food-growing to those with no more outside space than a windowsill or balcony.

Edible Landscaping is a method of introducing food into urban gardens. Common techniques include planting edible flowers, such as nasturtiums or daylilies, and adding fruit trees, berry bushes and fruiting vines.

Eutrophication refers to the over-enrichment of bodies of water, indicated by algae blooms that appear in streams, rivers, lakes and oceans as a result of fertilizer runoff or sewage discharge. It depletes the water's oxygen, killing fish and many other marine species and encouraging the growth of others, such as jellyfish.

Fairtrade (**Transfair** in Canada) is a branded version of the phrase "fair trade." In addition to indicating that the producers have been fairly compensated, it ensures that environmental, social and economic conditions have been met that benefit the producer's community.

Farmgate sales are food sales that take place at the farm; a farmgate price is the basic food price before marketing and mark-ups (the price of an item if sold by the farm).

Food Miles is a concept popularized in Canada by the authors of *The 100-Mile Diet*, Vancouver urbanites in search of a sustainable eating regime. It aims to measure the distance food travels from the point of production to the consumer's kitchen, and points out sustainability issues to do with fossil-fuel consumption and carbon emissions, as well as the costs in freshness, nutritional value and flavour incurred by long journeys.

Food Security is the condition of a population's adequate and assured access to safe, nutritious and appropriate food.

Food Sovereignty, a term coined by members

of **Via Campesina**, refers to the claimed "right" of peoples to define their own food, agriculture, livestock and fisheries systems, rather than being subject to the claims of international market forces over these.

Food Swaps are small, organized, community-based gatherings at which people meet their neighbours and trade foods they have grown, foraged and/or prepared.

Forest Gardening incorporates different vertical layers of plantings, mimicking the layers of food that might be found in a forest, from the tall canopy layer to ground plants and trailing vines.

Fruit Trees in city-dwellers' back yards or in abandoned orchards within cities are often left unharvested as people become too busy to attend to proper storage and preservation of the harvests. Initiatives like Not Far From the Tree (Toronto) and the Fruit Tree Project (Victoria) use volunteer labour to pick fruit and distribute it to urban food programs, or sell it to processors to fund food security programming.

Functional Foods contain elements (chemicals, cultures, vitamins etc.) that are intended to prevent or cure medical conditions. The term may be used for foods in their natural form – carrots and brazil nuts are examples – taken for their health properties, but it's more often used interchangeably with **Nutraceuticals**.

Gleaning Programs find ways to harvest unused urban fruit or the inevitable surplus food plants produced by farms or food gardens. In the latter case, when food is harvested for sale, there are often bruised, stunted or insect-damaged items that cannot be sold or given to food banks or charities because of their appearance and/or the time it would take to trim them in food preparation, but which are edible.

Good Food Boxes are a component of social programs found across Canada; they provide low-income people with bags or boxes of high-quality, fresh, nutritious foods at an affordable price.

Green Roofs are usually planted with non-edible ground cover to provide improved insulation and stormwater management, but they can be used for planting food gardens on rooftops, in containers, raised beds or other configurations. Buildings must be designed for the additional weight and drainage requirements, and many municipalities are incorporating guidelines and regulations to permit them. Such roofs offer cities additional benefits like improved air quality, rainwater management and insulation properties.

Green Walls (Living Walls) can be used for growing food. They offer buildings better insulation properties and improved air quality, although they must be planned with care to protect the building's envelope from water seepage, and to enable plant maintenance for aesthetic and harvesting purposes. Plants such as strawberries and grapevines are possibilities; more often green walls are decorative because of logistic problems in harvest.

Greenhouses are attractive growing options in Canada, where the northernmost populations are otherwise unable to grow fruits or vegetables. Even unheated greenhouses can be used to advantage in a snowy winter climate, as farmer-author Eliot Coleman has proven in Maine; in Iqaluit a disused ice rink has been converted to use for community food-growing. One issue concerning greenhouses is whether it's right to cover agricultural land with plastic and glass.

Guerilla Gardening is practiced by gardeners who wish to grow food as a public/political act. **Boulevards**, railway sidings and traffic circles are some of the spaces that have been taken over for this purpose. The food may be grown in untested and/or contaminated soil, so a guerilla garden is sometimes an act of protest rather than a functional garden.

Hotbeds are a largely forgotten method of generating heat for cold-frame food cultivation, a useful trick for a chilly winter. The Parisians were doing it back in the 19th century and earlier for their market gardens. It involves lining soil beds with composting straw and manure to keep the soil heated below a cold frame.

Hydroponics allows urbanites to grow food indoors using grow lights and water-based growing media. It's an alternative for those who lack soil, but it can be energy-intensive and call for chemical fertilizers, which are considered neither organic nor ideal for nutrient content of the plant products.

Lawn Farming: see **SPIN Farming**

Living Walls: see **Green Walls**.

Locavores are people who try to eat food produced locally and seasonally within an arbitrarily defined geographical area.

Nut Trees are often left out of urban forest planning on the grounds of nuisance or pest-control issues. Perversely, cities making such arguments have planted inedible horse chestnut trees, which have the same growing requirements as (edible) sweet chestnuts.

Nutraceuticals claim to combine the benefits of "nutrients" and "pharmaceuticals" by administering preventive or curative chemicals through food products.

Permaculture is a method of designing **Sustainable** gardens, modelled on nature. The concept was developed in Australia by Bill Mollison and David Holmgren and aims to reduce energy, water and waste through garden designs that engage natural processes.

Peri-urban refers to the outermost margins of a city, between its suburbs and the countryside. Many farms still exist in both peri-urban and **Suburban** areas, while the urban core swallows the surroundings: zoning changes, escalating real estate prices and lack of buffer areas can put these farms at great risk.

Pesticides are a hot topic in urban centres these days, and their use affects urban agriculture directly. Bowing to public pressure, some governments are moving to ban the cosmetic use of pesticides. Victoria has had such a bylaw since 2008; neighbouring Saanich introduced one in 2010; in 2009, Ontario banned the cosmetic use of 250 pesticides; and New Brunswick has restricted pesticide use but not banned it entirely.

Pollinators are vital to every method of food-growing. The honeybee – with its uncertain future worldwide – is only one example. Flies, wasps and other winged creatures in urban gardens are in equally precarious situations due to habitat loss and pesticide use.

School Gardens are increasingly popular in schools and post-secondary academic institutions of all kinds. In the US, Alice Waters, chef and locavore activist, became famous for the edible schoolyard projects she started. Slow Food in Nova Scotia launched an educational video called *Edible Schoolyard* in 2008.

Seed Swaps are a small-scale way to share the seeds from acclimatized plants within communities.

Seedy Saturdays are organized annual community seed swaps that allow local seed producers and home growers to buy, sell and trade local seeds.

SPIN (Small Plot Intensive) Farming (Lawn Farming) marshals unused backyards and turns them into productive urban farms or market gardens. The concept originated in Saskatoon and has spread widely.

Square-foot Gardening is a growing technique that allows intensive plantings in small spaces, ideal for urban gardens.

Suburban areas are the largely residential areas surrounding a city.

Sustainability in urban agriculture aims to create a growing system that minimizes "inputs" like soil, fertilizers and seed so that the farm or garden can be self-sufficient.

Truck Farms grow crops for sale to the public; food is grown on a commercial scale to be "trucked" into warehouses and distant markets.

Urban areas are built-up, built-on and usually fairly densely populated centres, featuring a mix of offices, industrial buildings and residences, regulated by a municipal government.

Urban Agriculture is any kind of activity that takes place within city limits, involving cultivation of soil, plants, fungi and animals to produce food and other products. It need not have a profit motive.

Urban Farming takes place within city limits, where plants and other agricultural food products are grown for personal use and/or for sale. Examples may include flower- and vegetable-raising, small-scale livestock (honey-bees, chickens), orchards and vineyards.

Vertical Gardens are grown vertically rather than horizontally, using **Green Walls** or other methods.

Via Campesina is a coalition of over 148 organizations that advocates family-farm-based sustainable agriculture and **Food Sovereignty**, a term that it originated.

BOOKSHELF

Ableman, Michael. *On Good Land: The Autobiography of an Urban Farm*. San Francisco: Chronicle Books, 1998.

Carpenter, Novella. *Farm City: The Education of an Urban Farmer*. New York: Penguin, 2009.

Cockrall-King, Jennifer. *Food and the City: Urban Agriculture and the New Food Revolution*. New York: Prometheus, 2012.

Coleman, Eliot. *The Winter Harvest Handbook*. White River Junction, VT: Chelsea Green, 2009.

Ehman, Amy Jo. *Prairie Feast: A Writer's Journey Home for Dinner*. Saskatoon, SK: Coteau, 2010.

Fraser, Evan D.G., and Andrew Rimas. *Empires of Food: Feast, Famine and the Rise and Fall of Civilizations*. Toronto: Simon and Schuster, Free Press, 2010.

Fukuoka, Masanobu. *The One-straw Revolution: An Introduction to Natural Farming*. Translated by Larry Korn, Chris Pearce, and Tsune Kurosawa. New York: New York Review of Books Classics, 2009.

Gardeners and Farmers of Terre Vivante, eds. *Keeping Food Fresh*. White River Junction, VT: Chelsea Green, 1999.

Gianfrancesco, Richard. *Grow Your Own Food*. London, UK: Apple Press, 2011.

Gibbons, Euell. *Stalking the Wild Asparagus*. Chambersburg, PA: Alan C. Hood & Company, 1962.

Halweil, Brian. *Eat Here: Reclaiming Homegrown Pleasures in a Global Supermarket*. New York: W.W. Norton, 2004.

Hart, Robert. *Forest Gardening: Cultivating an Edible Landscape*. White River Junction, VT: Chelsea Green, 1996.

Hemenway, Toby. *Gaia's Garden: A Guide to Home-scale Permaculture*, 2nd edition. White River Junction, VT: Chelsea Green, 2009.

Herriot, Carolyn. *The Zero-Mile Diet*. Madeira Park, BC: Harbour Publishing, 2010.

Hewitt, Ben. *The Town that Food Saved*. Emmaus, PA: Rodale, 2009.

Hobsbawn-Smith, dee. *Foodshed: An Edible Alberta Alphabet*. Victoria, BC: TouchWood, 2012.

Johnson, Lorraine. *City Farmer: Adventures in Urban Food Growing*. Vancouver, BC: Greystone, 2010.

Kingry, Judi, and Lauren Devine, eds. *Bernardin Guide to Home Preserving*. Richmond Hill, ON: Bernardin, 2003.

Ladner, Peter. *The Urban Food Revolution: Changing the Way We Feed Cities*. Gabriola Island, BC: New Society Publishers, 2011.

Lawrence, Felicity. *Not on the Label: What Really Goes into the Food on Your Plate*. New York: Penguin, 2004.

Lawrence, Felicity. *Eat Your Heart Out: Why the Food Business Is Bad for the Planet and Your Health*. New York: Penguin, 2008.

Nestle, Marion. *What to Eat*. New York: Macmillan, FSG Adult, 2007.

Nordahl, Darrin. *Public Produce: The New Urban Agriculture*. Washington, DC: Island Press, 2009.

Peacock, Paul. *The Urban Farmer's Handbook*. Preston, UK: Good Life Press, 2008.

Peterson, John. *Farmer John's Cookbook: The Real Dirt on Vegetables*. Layton, UT: Gibbs Smith, 2006.

Pollan, Michael. *The Omnivore's Dilemma: A Natural History of Four Meals*. New York: Penguin, 2006.

Pollan, Michael. *In Defense of Food: An Eater's Manifesto*. New York: Penguin, 2008.

de la Salle, Janine, and Mark Holland, eds. *Agricultural Urbanism: Handbook for Building Sustainable Food Systems in 21st Century Cities*. Winnipeg, MB: Green Frigate Books, 2010.

Singer, Peter, and Jim Mason. *The Way We Eat: Why Our Food Choices Matter*. Emmaus, PA: Rodale, 2006.

Smith, Alisa, and J.B. MacKinnon. *The 100-Mile Diet: A Year of Local Eating*. New York: Random House, 2007.

Standage, Tom. *An Edible History of Humanity*. New York: Walker & Company, 2009.

Steel, Carolyn. *Hungry City: How Food Shapes Our Lives*. New York: Vintage, 2009.

Tasch, Woody. *Inquiries into the Nature of Slow Money: Investing as if Food, Farms, and Fertility Mattered*. White River Junction, VT: Chelsea Green, 2008.

Tracey, David. *Urban Agriculture: Ideas and Designs for the New Food Revolution*. Gabriola Island, BC: New Society Publishers, 2011.

OTHER TITLES
IN THIS SERIES

Gift Ecology

Peter Denton

ISBN 978-1-927330-40-1

Little Black Lies

Corporate & Political Spin
in the Global War for Oil

Jeff Gailus

ISBN 978-1-926855-68-4

The Insatiable Bark Beetle

Dr. Reese Halter

ISBN 978-1-926855-67-7

The Incomparable Honeybee

and the Economics of Pollination
Revised & Updated

Dr. Reese Halter

ISBN 978-1-926855-65-3

The Beaver Manifesto

Glynnis Hood

ISBN 978-1-926855-58-5

The Grizzly Manifesto

In Defence of the Great Bear

by Jeff Gailus

ISBN 978-1-897522-83-7

Becoming Water

Glaciers in a Warming World

Mike Demuth

ISBN 978-1-926855-72-1

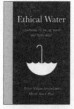

Ethical Water

Learning To Value What Matters Most

Robert William Sandford
& Merrell-Ann S. Phare

ISBN 978-1-926855-70-7

Denying the Source

The Crisis of First Nations Water Rights

Merrell-Ann S. Phare

ISBN 978-1-897522-61-5

The Weekender Effect

Hyperdevelopment in Mountain Towns

Robert William Sandford

ISBN 978-1-897522-10-3